The Art of **SERIES**
EDITED BY CHARLES BAXTER

D0058618

The Art of series is a line of books reinvigorating the practice of craft and criticism. Each book is a brief, witty, and useful exploration of fiction, nonfiction, or poetry by a writer impassioned by a singular craft issue. *The Art of* volumes provide a series of sustained examinations of key, but sometimes neglected, aspects of creative writing by some of contemporary literature's finest practitioners.

THE ART OF SUBTEXT

BEYOND PLOT

Other Books by Charles Baxter

NOVELS:

Saul and Patsy
The Feast of Love
Shadow Play
First Light

SHORT STORIES:

Gryphon: New and Selected Stories
Believers
A Relative Stranger
Through the Safety Net
Harmony of the World

NONFICTION:

Burning Down the House: Essays on Fiction

POETRY:

Imaginary Paintings

EDITOR:

Sherwood Anderson: Collected Stories
*Bringing the Devil to His Knees: The Craft of Fiction
    and the Writing Life* (co-editor Peter Turchi)
*A William Maxwell Portrait: Memories and
    Appreciations* (co-editors Michael Collier
    and Edward Hirsch)
Best New American Voices 2001
Graywolf Forum Three: The Business of Memory

The Art of

SUBTEXT

BEYOND PLOT

Charles Baxter

Graywolf Press

Publication of this volume is made possible in part by a grant provided by the Minnesota State Arts Board, through an appropriation by the Minnesota State Legislature; a grant from the Wells Fargo Foundation Minnesota; and a grant from the National Endowment for the Arts, which believes that a great nation deserves great art. Significant support has also been provided by the Bush Foundation; Target; the McKnight Foundation; and other generous contributions from foundations, corporations, and individuals. To these organizations and individuals we offer our heartfelt thanks.

Clara Ueland and Walt McCarthy are pleased to support the Graywolf Press "Art of" series in honor of Brenda Ueland.

Earlier versions of the essay "Inflection and the Breath of Life" have appeared in *Creating Fiction*, ed. Julie Checkoway (Story Press) and *Bringing the Devil to His Knees*, eds. Charles Baxter and Peter Turchi (University of Michigan Press); and a version of the essay "Loss of Face" first appeared in *The Believer*.

Published by Graywolf Press
250 Third Avenue North, Suite 600
Minneapolis, Minnesota 55401

www.graywolfpress.org

Published in the United States of America

ISBN 978-1-55597-473-2

6 8 10 12 13 11 9 7

Library of Congress Control Number: 2006938267

Series cover design: Scott Sorenson

Cover art: Scott Sorenson

Contents

For my students

THE ART OF SUBTEXT

BEYOND PLOT

Introduction

This brief book examines those elements that propel readers beyond the plot of a novel or short story into the realm of what haunts the imagination: the implied, the half-visible, and the unspoken. That subterranean realm with its overcharged psychological materials is often designated as the subtext of a story. To discuss subtexts at first appears to be a hopelessly contradictory mission. It's like saying, "I am about to show you how to show the unseen." Or: "I wish to demonstrate how to think about the unthinkable."

Between stagings and subtexts a bewildering relation seems to exist. Writers must often use a staggering amount of surface bric-a-brac to suggest an indistinct presence underneath that surface. The stronger the presence of the unspoken and unseen, the more gratuitous details seem to be required, a proliferation that signifies a world both solid and haunted. What is displayed evokes what is *not* displayed, like a party where the guests discuss, at length, those who are not in attendance. In this context the word "haunted" is probably apt. Our most haunting dreams, no matter how hallucinatory, are the most busily etched. The details themselves signal belief-weight, the gravity of a vision that can't be shrugged off—think of the hyperdetailing in Hieronymus Bosch's *The Garden of Earthly Delights,* to take one example from visual art. That table in a nightmare comes complete with a frightening particularity. Its solidity and substance—its black sheen, its *five* asymmetrical corners, its immovable weight—attest to conviction and a kind of interior truth.

In fiction, the half-visible and the unspoken—all those subtextual matters—are evoked when the action and dialogue of the scene angle downward, when by their multiplicity they imply as much as they show. A slippery surface causes you to skid into the subtext.

To take the reader into that critical twilight zone, that landscape haunted by the unseen, I have sought to illustrate the way the subtext—the unspoken soulmatter—is evoked in a story by discussing how characters reveal themselves through dramatic placement ("The Art of Staging"); what subtexts are made of and how they're brought to the surface ("Digging the Subterranean"); how fiction writers pay attention to the way people no longer pay attention ("Unheard Melodies"); how inflections take us, by means of tonal shifts, out of the literal and into the metaphorical and the suggestive ("Inflection and the Breath of Life"); how characters lose their surface-level self-possession ("Creating a Scene"); and, finally, how the face serves as a semi-reliable guide to those subsurface feelings whenever the mask appears to fall, or to fail ("Loss of Face"). Writers on the lookout for practical advice might find these examples suggestive, or, with luck, inspiring.

For the most part, I've chosen examples from fiction with which most readers should be familiar. And my critical approach has a certain retro quality here and there. In my earlier book of critical essays, *Burning Down the House,* I was eager to reintroduce an element of performative drama into criticism—criticism, the dreariest of the arts—by means of unsubstantiated generalizations and half-legitimated claims asserted at high volume. Here it seemed best to perform a few close readings, acting out the role of the critic-as-sleuth. The close readings seemed unavoidable in a discussion of texts haunted by their subtexts. Think of these essays, then, as the reports of a private investigator, examining a few stories with a magnifying glass, looking for the secret panel, the hidden stairway, the lovingly concealed dungeon, and the ghosts moaning from beneath the floor.

The Art of Staging

Books sometimes fall into your hands in the oddest ways. Meeting up with a particular work of literature may have an eeriness of occasion that resembles an accident that is not really accidental. Bernardo Atxaga's novel *Obabakoak,* for instance, was recommended to me late one night in a Barcelona restaurant after much conversation and a great deal of wine. I wrote down this curious title on a sodden piece of paper and put it into my wallet. For the next month, every time I tried to get out some dollar bills or a picture ID, my note with the stuttering cryptic word "Obabakoak" printed on it would drop out and fall to the floor. Time and again, I would pick it up and put it back into my wallet. Time and again, the piece of paper, still smelling of wine, would reappear. After some hunting on the web—the book is out of print in the United States—I finally obtained a copy, and soon after I did, the piece of paper obligingly disappeared from my wallet.

Obabakoak is a wonderfully peculiar novel. Written originally in the Basque language and published in 1988, then translated into Spanish by the author and subsequently translated from its Spanish version into English by Margaret Jull Acosta and published in this country by Pantheon in 1992, it was yanked out of print a few years later. Such was the obstacle course in the American literary marketplace for a book whose specialty is a kind of intimate, wry muttering. (One of its chapter headings is titled, "How to Plagiarize.") Early on in *Obabakoak*—the title refers to the goings-on in the Basque village of Obaba—we are introduced to a character named Esteban Werfell. At the same time and in the same paragraph we are also introduced to the library where he writes. Esteban is a literary type, and he is surrounded on all four walls by about twelve thousand leather-bound volumes, some of them his own purchases and some of them his father's.

In this room, among all these books, there is one window.

> . . . a window through which, while he wrote, Esteban Werfell could see the sky, the willows, the lake and the little house built there for the swans in the city's main park. Without really impinging on his solitude, the window made an inroad into the darkness of the books and mitigated that other darkness which often creates phantoms in the hearts of men who have never quite learned how to live alone.

Esteban's inner life is singularly like the room in which he sits. The parallelism is exact. The scene includes two complementary darknesses, the first a non-metaphorical darkness and the second being "that other darkness," the shadowy psychic world of Esteban Werfell's self-imposed imaginative conditioning that he shares with other men "who have never quite learned how to live alone." This community defined by solitude invites a party of phantasms and should be familiar to most writers and readers as the locale of emotional and cognitive associations. The literal window makes an "inroad" on the literal darkness, and its view of willows and lake and swan house eases Esteban's soul without touching his isolation. The willows and the sky and the swan house constitute the prisoner's portion, his meager diet of the real. (A recent Nobel Prize–winner in literature, Orhan Pamuk, claimed in his Nobel speech that such rooms are shared by all writers, everywhere.)

Esteban's room serves as that classic enclosure, the haunt of the imagination. This site can be a mental or a physical place or both at once. Alfred, Lord Tennyson's Lady of Shalott lived there until she grew "half sick of shadows," broke her mirror and became, in effect, a Victorian zombie sleepwalking her way to her watery death. Honoré de Balzac apocryphally chained to his desk, Marcel Proust in his cork-lined room, Lord Chandos in his castle, Jorge Luis Borges in his library, Emily Dickinson behind her closed shutters, Plato's inhabitants of the cave—all of them inhabit prisons where the imagination is doomed to flourish.

As an allegory of the world of appearances, Plato's cave is also an enclosure of sorts where the receptive imagination is called upon to make some narrative sense of the shadows on the wall. Plato's cave is a libelous accusation against art itself. Plato generally mistrusted art as the evil twin of philosophy and goes to great lengths to say so in Book Three of *The Republic*, but through a kind of indeliberate dramatic irony, art arises in Plato's cave as comfort and compensation. The world of appearances has a trapdoor that takes you into a counterworld of meaningful dreams. Plato's cave—I knew of a film society with this name, and, more recently, a tattoo parlor—was one of the first undergrounds devoted to visions. Not entirely by accident, it resembles a theater.

An image of the writerly mind walled up among books with one window looking fixedly outward: this is where Atxaga's novel begins, and it is the model for the apparent division of the literal and the associational, the textual and the subtextual. We are presented with a man and the staging area of his life, along with the imprisoning rewards of his bookish work. Outside and inside, object and metaphor, are somehow reciprocal. The picture of the object—what I'd call the pictorialism—leads by a circuitous route to the inner life. In this passage the separation between the soul of the world and the body in which that soul is housed has melted away.

This is like saying that the paintings that seem most like dreams—those by Giorgio de Chirico or René Magritte or Max Ernst, for example—also have a strange and seemingly unnecessary accumulation of detail, a chronic fixation in which it is dangerous to move in any direction. Something has been frozen in place.

Esteban's library and this novel, *Obabakoak,* constitute both the blockade and the window, the dungeon and the escape route. The room, after all, is not yet sealed up. Light streams in through the glass like the light from a projectionist's booth. We can't see the swans, but thanks to the reference to their shelter, they're there by implication, as is much else in this novel.

These passages invite the reader into a kind of productive daydreaming, but for an American reader the language has arrived by two removes and is therefore only an approximation of what the writer intended.

Nevertheless, what struck me immediately about this passage was its dramatic staging. I knew where I was and where the main character was sitting. I also knew his situation and something about his emotional life. With nervous gratified shock I *recognized* the room and the metaphor it created, and I had a needling suspicion that Esteban Werfell's story would have something to do with mistaking shadows for real things—as, in fact, it does, with a fallen idealist as its main character. In the careful evocation of a subtext, a writer would, hypothetically, learn, step by step, how to create an interior space, using details of location and objects that mirror a psychological condition.

Reading the passage from Atxaga for the first time, I myself sat in a windowless basement room. The novel may have been written originally in Basque, but I know Esteban's scene well enough. I am writing these words now in a similar room. The walls are lined (is "insulated" the right word?) with books. The room's only source of natural light is a section of the ceiling where three square pieces of "ballroom glass"—glass in the upstairs floor—permit the sun's light to penetrate for a few hours a day from the upstairs window, but only in midsummer. This is my palace, my prison cell, my library, my empire, my haunt, my own theatrical staging area, this room.

To use the word "staging" in relation to literary fiction sounds like a beginner's mistake. Staging, it seems reasonable to think, applies only to the theatrical stage. When I told a brilliantly intelligent writer friend with a dozen acclaimed novels to her credit that I was writing a meditation on staging, she wrote back to ask, "What is staging?"

So in my next letter I cited Gretta Conroy transfixed on the staircase landing at the end of the evening as she listens to Bartell D'Arcy singing "The Lass of Aughrim," while downstairs in the middle of the front hallway Gabriel Conroy gazes in rapt attention at her. Gabriel watches; Gretta listens; offstage, Bartell D'Arcy can be heard, by implication. No one moves. There is a chain of four acts of attention, if you include the reader's attention to Gabriel, and the attention keeps going up the stairs, ascending. This moment near the end of James Joyce's "The Dead" is intensely dramatic, and yet for all its drama it is quite static.

Staging in fiction involves putting characters in specific strategic positions in the scene so that some unvoiced nuance is revealed. Staging may include how close or how far away the characters are from each other, what their particular gestures and facial expressions might be at moments of dramatic emphasis, exactly how their words are said, and what props appear inside or outside. Excessive detailing is its signpost. Certainly it involves the writer in the stagecraft of her characters just as a director would, blocking out the movement of the actors. Staging might be called *the micro-detailing implicit in scene-writing when the scene's drama intensifies and takes flight out of the literal into the unspoken.* It shows us how the characters are behaving, and it shows us what they cannot say through the manner in which they say what they *can* say. Staging gives us a glimpse of their inner lives, what is in their hearts, just as Esteban Werfell's study leads us also to his soul. Staging, you might argue, is the poetry of action and setting when it evokes the otherwise unstated.

For years I was puzzled by the phenomena of airport/airplane reading. The spectacle of people reading before and during flights wasn't especially perplexing, but what always baffled me was the narrowness of the selections. Walk down the aisle of almost any airplane and you are likely to see passengers hunched up, bent over, the men reading Tom Clancy novels and the women reading Danielle Steel novels. I am exaggerating here, but not to a criminal degree.

The techno-political thriller and the romance novel are similar in their preoccupation with procedural issues related to material objects. But they aren't "staged" in the way I am using that word because they have virtually no interest in using dramatic means to reveal character and the inner life. Instead, they provide materially overdetermined hypernarratives that aim to reduce the scale of human beings in relation to the things that surround them.

In a Tom Clancy novel, we are presented with details of military hardware, hierarchies of power, both military and civilian, and a loose cannon to set the plot into motion. The loose cannon is always required to destabilize things-as-they-are. In any particular scene the writing locates the characters quickly, but then characterizes the hardware *at length.* In these novels human beings can be summarized with almost embarrassing ease. They have roles to play, which they perform well or badly. (Conveniently, however, they have no souls.) The hardware, by contrast, is unimaginably complex and requires considerable writerly hubbub. In fact the hardware takes on the sex appeal that the characters typically lack. The only element left in doubt is the outcome of the plot, not the vagaries of human nature. The characteristic resolution to a novel of this type is a return to the status quo, with the addition of a new regulatory agency.

Similarly, in a romance novel the exotic location and the details of material wealth eventually lead the reader to an understanding of who is profitably to be paired off with whom. The imaginative energy devoted to hardware in the techno-political thriller is applied here to clothing, sex appeal, accessories, the sovereignty of riches, location (the more exotic the better), physical attributes, and lifestyle choices. In a romance novel a disturbance to social hierarchies may be settled through marriage or a cunning liaison. Men once thought to be mysterious and dangerous can be understood and tamed through sex, domestic affection, and familial ties. The characteristic resolution to this sort of novel is a marriage and the displacement of a threatening female figure to the distant background, usually a cemetery.

Both kinds of novels are fully explicit about human nature, which, though more complex in the romance novel than in the techno-political thriller, must be revealed by the novel's end. *Things* are celebrated and given an aura. The aura around a thing is a good sign of commodity culture busily at work. Both genres are absolutely opposed to ongoing mystery and to the unknowable. Everything that needs to be said can and will be said. As a result, these books leave very little to the imagination to reconstruct. And both kinds of novels indulge in material overstatement—a knowingness about objects thought to be valuable, along with a fascination with technique, the exact way to do something properly—making love, mixing a martini, or firing off a torpedo.

The techno-political thriller and the romance novel serve as antidotes to the imagination rather than stimulants to it. For this reason they make for ideal reading in airports and airplanes. They effectively shut down the imagination by doing all its work for it. They leave the spirit or the soul—and ambiguity, for that matter—out of the equation. By shutting down the imagination, genre novels perform a useful service to the anxious air traveler by reducing his or her ability to speculate. For the most part, people on airplanes, and here I include myself, would rather not use their speculative imaginations at all; one consequence of this situation is that great poetry is virtually unreadable during turbulence, when the snack cart has been put away and the seat belts fastened. Enough anxiety is associated with air travel without Rainer Maria Rilke's *Sonnets to Orpheus* making it worse.

Both the techno-political thriller and the romance novel can be understood as replicas of certain features of American culture. Robert Hass once noticed that the separation between objects and the inner life defined a quarrel Robert Bly carried on against modernism decades ago. Bly was all for giving up the representation of material life in pursuit of the soul, in the form of the deep poetic image. A kind of polarization of content was therefore suggested. The fixation on material objects and the distrust of the spirit or the soul produce in genre fiction a no-man's-land where everything has a price tag, but where a character like Esteban Werfell, his library, and Bernardo Atxaga's *Obabakoak* itself would have no place and no value. The soul, or "the soul," placed under suspicion and quotation marks, becomes a refugee with no known habitation or refuge. In their particular form of material insistence, genre novels depend upon the management of mannequin characterization and reassuringly recognizable types from whom the complexity of humanity and all questions related to the soul have conveniently leaked out.

When objects and actions create a pathway to the spirit, to a character's inner life, you are in the presence of "staging" as I am defining it here—a balancing between the concrete and the unutterable. It is all reciprocal. Staging is compatible with poetry in a way that material overstatement never can be. Staging implies mystery by dramatizing the gestures we make in its direction.

The staged poem

The contemporary reaction against narrative devices in poetry has been so belligerent that associating staging with poetry sounds like a radically rearguard act. Perhaps also a rather stupid one, at that. Nevertheless, some of the genius of great poetry has at times involved the logic of staging the unspoken—*Paradise Lost,* to name one obvious example. What often makes dramatic poems memorable is the effect of the narrative close-up on chillingly ambiguous action in league with abnormal psychology, as in the work of the contemporary poet B. H. Fairchild. When describing behavior, certain poets of the dramatic lyric have quite happily staged the domestic theater of wounded egos. Robert Frost, to cite one example, was a better domestic psychologist and dramatist than most of the fiction writers of his generation. Savage household quarrels were mother's milk to him.

For example, here are the well-known opening lines of Frost's "Home Burial," a dramatic lyric. Imagine this stanza as a series of stage directions in which the characters' hidden feelings suddenly arise through gesture alone. We are given a plot, and then, very rapidly, we move beyond it by means of hyperdetailing.

> He saw her from the bottom of the stairs
> Before she saw him. She was starting down,
> Looking back over her shoulder at some fear.
> She took a doubtful step and then undid it
> To raise herself and look again. He spoke
> Advancing toward her: 'What is it you see
> From up there always—for I want to know.'
> She turned and sank upon her skirts at that,
> And her face changed from terrified to dull.
> He said to gain time: 'What is it you see,'

> Mounting until she cowered under him.
> 'I will find out now—you must tell me, dear.'
> She, in her place, refused him any help
> With the least stiffening of her neck and silence.
> She let him look, sure that he wouldn't see,
> Blind creature; and awhile he didn't see.
> But at last he murmured, 'Oh,' and again, 'Oh.'

This is a brilliantly—if acidly—observed domestic scene that many long-term couples would probably recognize. Almost every device of staging is visible here in the service of what the woman, Amy, and her husband cannot or will not say to each other, behind the screen of what they actually do say. It is not that actions speak louder than words; they speak *instead* of words.

The scene begins in a cramped space: the two characters cannot physically avoid each other, always a profitable situation for a dramatist, who should be on the lookout for opportunities to crowd the characters, cram them into insufficient quarters. Frost notes that Amy is located above her husband on the stairs, a place where she prefers to be, but she is distracted, with the result that he sees her before she sees him. The physical staging thus gives her an advantage (she can look down at her husband), but her husband's ability to catch her unobserved gives him an advantage too, particularly in those two areas where he is thought to be obtuse: first, his ability to register what he is seeing, and second, his timing.

The language of the poem is resolutely concrete until the third line's "some fear," a fear that is apparent in Amy's facial expression (the scene is initially from the husband's point of view) and also apparent in her distracted stutter-step downward and then back up again. The governing emotion—her fear—is extrapolated from her expression and gestures. In the manner of an Ernest Hemingway story, Frost's micro-detailing indicates where these two characters are looking and the way in which those glances reflect the two characters' unspoken thoughts. Their refusal to speak directly reflects both the pain of the subject and the wife's contempt for and fear of her husband.

When the husband begins to speak, the narrative lets us know that he is "advancing toward her," an action accompanying his speech that in itself seems threatening. It is as if he has to use his hulking physical presence to emphasize his words, overpower his wife, and extract some sort of answer from her. Following his question, really more a demand than a question, the poem immediately crosscuts to her reaction, which is to sit down, an act of temporizing that stops his advance and keeps her height advantage on the stairway over him. She does not say anything here. She replies to his question with a silence that is more a commentary on *him* than on the challenge he has flung at her. A silence suggests a demand that's not worth answering. Her face (Frost is not above describing facial reactions—he has at times an unseemly interest in them) moves from "terrified to dull," and most readers will infer that she has used this expression on him more than once, a dull expression to match the dullness of the man she finds herself married to.

To "gain time"—the husband is flustered by her strategic silence and by her sitting down—he repeats his question, but in a different form. In a fight, timing is everything: he needs a moment to regroup his thoughts. Meanwhile he continues to use his physical body to intimidate her, approaching so closely to where she is sitting that she "cower[s]" under him. She has lost the advantage she once had in elevation. In the poetry of cramped quarters and resentful silences, Frost shows the reader exactly where the two bodies are lined up in physical space and how those bodies also constitute a form of address, a private physical language that couples share: passive and reacting though implicitly superior on her part, powerful and active but inarticulate, inferior, and seemingly insensitive on his.

More micro-detailing: with "the least stiffening of her neck," she makes an intimate wife-to-husband gesture that I take to mean, "Look up at the window." She's nodding, that is, in the window's direction. It's not clear that she believes he'll get it. A long, pained history between the two of them is therefore implied. But to her surprise he *does* get it. Maybe he isn't as dumb as she thinks he is. The point of view has meanwhile shifted over to her, so that her judgment of him as a "blind creature" may enter the poem. His behavior now actively contradicts her assumptions about him. Apparently she's mistaken about his blindnesses. He is able to see as well as look. The word "see" is highlighted three times in this passage by being placed in an end-stopped position. When he does gaze upward, he says "Oh" not once but twice, the first "Oh" signifying that he has realized that the family cemetery is outside that window, and the second "Oh" that their son is there, and that *this* is what her silences are all about.

Something about this death is what she holds against him. He has guessed what it is and possibly understands it as a salted wound. I hear the second "Oh" as quieter and lower in pitch than the first, in my own line reading of the scene. The double insight is marked by this doubled exclamation, which marks a split second's painful recognition, and it also marks what is haunting these two, the body and soul of their absent child. It is as if an element out of Gothic narrative has moved inside and has been translated into a domestic quarrel. The Gothic element surfaces in many, if not most, of

Frost's poems, most notably "The Hill Wife," and "Two Witches." There is an odd, creaking haunted-house ingredient in many of these poems that puts them into the strange subcategory of horror-poetry.

In real time, this scene would take about twenty-five seconds to enact. But Frost's notation of detail here extends the implications of the scene so that its anguish seems interminable and repetitive, incapable of resolving itself or becoming subject to a catharsis. This traumatized couple has had a death imprinted on them psychologically and re-enacted through painstakingly notated gestures, like an endlessly replayed psychological loop that cannot get free of its own repetitions.

The entire episode is about the unseen and the unarticulated. Every action these two perform points to what is missing for them, the gap that the spark of their resentment and rage seeks to cross. These two could be any couple finding themselves blocking each other in any hallway and starting up a bitter argument before they've even found the right words or, for that matter, a subject for their argument. They have initiated a quarrel before they are ready for it and are therefore confounded by what they find themselves doing and saying. The scene, after many re-readings, still feels nervously alive, perhaps because this couple seems to have been thrown out of time altogether—they will quarrel like this forever.

Frost's commitment to his characters' inner lives becomes apparent through the poem's calmly fevered hyperdetailing. This poet is dreadfully patient whenever fixation is his subject. By giving up grand abstractions from the start, "Home Burial" arrives at the soul's secret chamber through the obsessively literal. This door to the chamber is obvious to everyone. What is not so obvious is how to open it. Oddly, it often requires someone who is laconic or taciturn, a person whose very refusal to go directly to the heart of the matter prolongs the anguish and thereby forces it to appear.

We find this element also in the work of a contemporary short-story writer, Richard Bausch. Bausch's beautiful, harrowing stories stand against the truism that if people simply *talk* about their problems with sufficient eloquence, the problems will solve themselves. In Bausch's stories, talking first exacerbates the problem and then becomes the problem, like a medicine that in high doses acquires toxicity. Dialogue, instead of bringing people together, instead tends to define their differences and then casts those differences in stone. Despite their loquacity, Bausch's characters can never talk about what they actually want or need; there is always a guardrail around introspection. Many of his stories are therefore composites of two stories, the story going on now and the one that lies out somewhere in the past and that serves as the background, unreachable, and which in any case is almost always too volatile or poisonous to handle directly. The story in the foreground serves as what I will call the "staging area," where we witness the gradual uprising of what has gone unsaid. As a consequence, Bauschean stories are almost ritually haunted by the inexpressible.

The writerly strategy here is complex but not complicated. You put in the foreground, the staging area, the story that is going on now. This story gradually reveals what has happened in the past, where the chronic tensions are, and whose echoes are still audible.

For example, in the astonishing "What Feels Like the World," the staging consists of a few hours in the day, beginning in the morning when Brenda, an overweight middle-schooler, is first seen jumping rope, trying to get into shape for a public school assembly that evening, when all the members of her class will be vaulting over a gymnastics horse, one by one, in a public display. So far, Brenda has been unable to do this vault and is the only member of her class who will risk this terrible public humiliation. The witness to this, her guardian, is her grandfather, the story's central protagonist. But the story is not really about Brenda's vault, exactly. Its subject is the afterlife of unexpressed sorrow: Brenda's mother, we learn, in a slow unraveling of facts, has died in an automobile accident that may well have been a suicide (Brenda's father has also abandoned her), and both Brenda and her grandfather are preoccupied with that death, which is almost, though not quite, beyond expression.

The burden Brenda's grandfather has taken on is to persuade Brenda that her mother has not deliberately abandoned her. "An accident is an accident," he insists. Beyond this denial, his solution for grief is to pretend that it doesn't exist. Denial is thus piled on denial.

> He pretends to her that he's still going on to work in the mornings after he walks her to school, because he wants to keep her sense of the daily balance of things, of a predictable and ordinary routine, intact. He believes this is the best way to deal with grief—simply to go on with things, to keep them as much as possible as they have always been.

A strategy of this sort creates, almost in spite of itself, the huge energy of negation that radiates in all narrative directions, like a headache that seems to blossom *inside* the world that the sufferer is forced to observe. The metaphor the story finds for such denial is, appropriately, a heart attack. "They're used to the absence of her mother by now—it's been almost a year—but they still find themselves missing a beat now and then, like a heart with a valve almost closed."

The grandfather has his own problems, which, given the tyrannical logic of his various disavowals, are also unarticulated. He has recently lost his job, is going broke, and of course hasn't told Brenda. Again and again, the grandfather knows that he might say the word, "make his way through to her grief." But he lacks both the strength and the will to do so, and in any case his own anguish blocks all avenues of expression. All his talk masks his *in*articulated preoccupations and somehow intensifies them. This creates a stalemate effect that puts the dramatic pressure on the staging area and on the story's conclusion, when Brenda is about to attempt the vault. Standing "in a doorway, her cheeks flushed, her legs looking too heavy in the tights," she scans the crowd for her grandfather, for a witness to what she's about to do. She stands in a frozen tableau of suffering and adolescent forlornness.

> It's as if she were merely curious as to who is out there, but he knows she's looking for him, searching the crowd for her grandfather, who stands on his toes, unseen against the far wall, stands there thinking his heart might break, lifting his hand to wave.

This beautiful ending comprises the last dramatic movement of the story, where two desolate gestures (Brenda's search for her grandfather's face, and the grandfather's wave) meet each other in midair, the only successful vault in the story. Every alert reader will have already guessed that Brenda will fail at this test and every test the school gives her. The story's true subject, unexpressed grief, exists behind the walls of the visible world, and in that sense the story is already over and has been over ever since it (apparently) started. In this theater of muted damaged characters, what Brenda actually does or does not do no longer matters. Her suffering blocks out all possibility for taking the next step, whatever the size. No matter how large or small the physical vault that Brenda has been asked to perform, she will stumble, and her grandfather will have to witness it, both of them in their fixed positions.

Imagine a quarrel as seen by a frightened but very intelligent and observant child. The frightened child is certain that whatever is going on will result in some change in the way he himself is treated. The frightened child is thus in a condition of full attentiveness, of certainty combined with incomplete information and emotional bewilderment. The suspense he feels is unpleasant and stressful and charged with meaning. Because he does not know which details to look at, he must look at them all, and his hallucinated attention will cause those details to expand with a sort of terrible visionary energy.

Whenever people are saying and doing strange things, an ability to observe and interpret these curiosities may be a life-or-death matter. Henry James's novels, Stanley Kunitz's poems, and many of Edward P. Jones's stories and Paula Fox's novels often start from this strategic narrative locale.

The frightened child is one model for an ideal observer of a dramatic scene. The unguided insecure foreigner in a hostile country might be another. The would-be lover half-dying of desire might be a third such observer because such lovers are fixated on details that have bloomed with an ecstatic and occasionally menacing force.

"To make anything interesting," Gustave Flaubert said, "you simply have to look at it long enough." What if you have to look at it for *too* long? These hypervigilant observers—the frightened child, the unguided foreigner, the half-dying lover, and a broken couple like the one in the Frost poem—are forced through desperate circumstances to gaze upon the world in an abnormally attentive way. They are beyond plot. They are in pursuit of meanings that words and objects will yield to when used as means but not as ends. We are not accustomed to look at the world in this fixated way, and the effect is beautiful, bewildering, frightening, and, at times, comic.

Literature is often born out of baffling physical details, an overabundance that tells us that the world's surface is readable only when we don't quite know how to pose the right question to it. In not knowing how to look and not knowing what to say, we begin to fixate on the constituent materials and find ourselves diving under the surface, down to the substratum of art.

Digging the Subterranean

When I was a boy, I used to play a Parker Brothers' board game called *Careers.* The premise of *Careers* was quite ingenious, though difficult to describe to those unfamiliar with it. Before the players started moving around on the game board, they each had to decide which of three life-goals they wanted most—money, fame, or love—and in what proportion. The goals had to be quantified to add up to sixty points. You could try to get your sixty points in only one category such as love, or you could hedge your bets and try to get different quantities of the three categories that would add up to sixty. But you couldn't win if you got rewards that you hadn't asked for. You could only win if you *got* what you had said you *wanted.*

For example, you could be cautious and set up your contract with life to consist of twenty points of fame, twenty points of money, and twenty points of love. Or you could go for broke for love, saying before the game started that you were out for love and love only, sixty points of love, nothing but love. But then in order to win you had to *get* sixty points of love as you traveled around the game board. You had to land on the love squares and accumulate the love-points. If you landed on the fame or the money squares, the points would do you no good at all because you had gone into the game wanting love and nothing but love. Fame was irrelevant to your goals.

I sometimes played this game with a neighbor kid whose parents had a great deal of money. When he played *Careers* he nearly always wanted money, usually fifty points worth of money, and about ten points worth of fame to make up the difference. He never wanted love. He thought only girls wanted love. (We were eleven years old.) He wanted money and fame because he thought that was what men should want, and he'd curse whenever he landed on the love-squares. I wonder what happened to him—as an adult, I mean. I heard that he ended up in jail for a while for drug dealing.

In its game-board way *Careers* was accurate about life-choices and about certain features of narrative. The shadow truth of *Careers* is that what you ask for in life is not necessarily what you get. As it turns out, the discrepancy between what you ask for and what you get constitutes a story and not a game. You can ask for money and get love instead. You can ask for fame and get nothing but money. You can ask for all three and not get much of anything. Depending on how you view these matters, to ask for certain outcomes in life and to get another result is tragic or comic or some combination of the two, depending on where the observer is standing.

Much of the time you can say whatever you wish to say about what you want. But you can't always say aloud what you really crave or desire because for some reason it's unmentionable. You want the wrong thing, or too much of it. These discrepancies are at the core of many great stories, and myths. Think of Oedipus, famous forever for wanting the wrong thing, and getting it.

Young writers tend to hate the whole idea of plot. A plot feels like entrapment, or, even worse, commitment. Any plot will close down certain options. It thus resembles the aging process. In some respects, plot springs directly from our characters' desires or their fears and what they are willing to do to fulfill those desires or to avoid the objects of their fears. It can be imagined as a chain-bridge with a chasm underneath it, a linkage of cause and effect with that abyss visible below. As it happens, there are not all that many things to want deeply, at least if you believe the evidence of *Careers.* The categories stay the same while the variable instances change. The beauty and surprise reside in the instances. A novel is not a summary of its plot but a collection of instances, of luminous specific details that take us in the direction of the unsaid and unseen.

After all, most people want some kind of identity. When they're young, they often want some adventures (in other words, they want to get out of the house), and as they get older, they want some peace and stability (in other words, they want to get back *into* the house). They want love, sometimes too much of it, or sex (ditto), or marriage and children. They want money. They want to know the meaning of things. They want a life of the spirit or a life of the body or both. They want to avoid painful situations, unless they are good at creating painful situations and then watching others deal with them. Just about everything else they want can be included in one of these categories.

All these wants provide the starting point for plots. As Peter Brooks observes in his book *Reading for the Plot*, in the absence of desires, stories remain stillborn. My invented fictional character may want money, or sex or love, or whatever it may be, and is willing to go somewhere in order to achieve that goal. Perhaps my character is wracked with fears and must face up to adverse circumstances or an antagonist or two. We therefore have some resistance to her plans or goals or strategies. Perhaps something happens to him or her, and s/he reacts in a certain way. As a result, the story contains two or three acts. Without a mobilized desire or fear, characters in a story—or life—won't be willing to do much of anything in the service of their great longings and phobias that take over the visible world.

A certain kind of story does not depend so much on what the characters say they want as what they actually want but can't own up to. This inability to be direct creates a subterranean chasm within the story, where genuine desires hide beneath the superficial ones. The conflict here begins with the self, not the world. Another kind of story depends on the discrepancy between what the characters have wanted and what they actually get. This state of affairs creates a kind of poetic irony that the world has bestowed on the character. The first kind of story, the unspeakable-subtext story, often arises whenever characters appear to be in the grip of some kind of obsessional and often unspoken mania. A mania creates what I want to call a *congested* subtext, and often the best interests of a story are served when the subtext is as congested as possible. The emotions and the meanings in the story go off in every possible direction and remain in the mind long after the story is over. I'm using the word "congested" here to suggest a complex set of desires and fears that can't be efficiently described, a pile-up of emotions that resists easy articulation.

Having a mania does not make a person into a maniac. There are civilized and domesticated manias: coin collecting, stamp collecting, model trains, lawn care. Having an obsession may be part of everyday life (sports, knitting, politics). Mania: an emotional over-investment in any object that can't possibly give back what the individual wants from it. Obsessions and manias are narrative-friendly, partly because maniacs draw attention to themselves. The spectacle of fixation has a quality of contagion: it is hard not to pay attention to obsessives. Except for adolescent infatuations, which are *too* everyday, there's nothing like a good usable obsession to provide an interesting story. Anytime someone, real or imaginary, stands shivering in the fever of obsessive fixation, that figure serves as a possible source for a story if that character can stay seemingly calm and rational on the outside, and if the obsession has some resonance in the culture as a whole.

Such characters serve as *focusing agents* for the entire story. You can't take your eyes off them. A story without a focusing agent is a bit like a painting without a center of interest.

Consider *Moby-Dick*. The novel's central figure is a wounded, self-dramatizing, and obsessive sea captain, Captain Ahab, and the plot concerns his pursuit of the eponymous White Whale in Ahab's ship, the *Pequod*.

But to summarize the plot of this novel is to say almost nothing about the book. *Moby-Dick* is a frightening, memorable, and puzzling novel in part because its subtext is so overloaded, and because, once onstage, Ahab demands our attention. Despite his eloquence, Ahab in some fundamental way cannot explain himself. He cannot quite articulate what drives him to his personal extremes. He doesn't know why he needs to kill the whale, but he does know that he has to enlist the entire crew of his ship in his project. His wound is larger than his missing leg—Ahab is *all* wound, all rage against the universe created by a blank, indifferent God. Nothing that Ahab says is adequate to the wound. The novel, finally, seeks the source of that wound but does not find it, though it seems to find evidence of something else in every corner where its gaze happens to fall.

Mania always enlarges its object. Moby-Dick, the whale, is of great size, but this animal takes on gigantic, metaphysical proportions as the object of Ahab's attention.

Ahab's obsession with this masklike, unreadable whale is both weirdly out of proportion and hugely significant. Ahab is a representative figure: a crazed, charismatic leader. His overdetermined goals move out of the practical and the personal into the metaphysical, the spiritual, the psychosexual, and the political.

Herman Melville's novel stands in awe of Ahab's mania, and every effort to get at him and at the object of his obsession redirects the story and the action to the climactic calamity. Ahab takes almost the entire ship down with him. Everyone but Ishmael dies, thanks to Ahab's folly. Obsession and congested subtexts have a tendency to enmesh and co-opt innocent bystanders, who have only common sense with which to combat mania. In the war of common sense and mania, mania always wins the first few rounds. Fanatics have both drama and conviction on their side.

Obsessions—ill-defined though they may be—breed collaborators, and they turn personal subjects into collective cultural subjects. Under the burden of obsession, plots enlarge in significance. Ensnaring all bystanders, they acquire sociopolitical meanings and counter-meanings. Every fixated leader who resists rational discourse, from Ahab down to our current legislators, has contempt for those who are "reality-based."

Ahab does not and cannot tell his own story. As a narrator, he would be not only unreliable but inadequate *even* if he survived the story; in any case, the maniac seldom survives his own story. A person navigating through a congested subtext rarely has the self-possession to tell a story, and therefore he or she needs a witness, and that's why we have Ishmael, our narrator-companion. Ishmael is our tour-guide to the *Pequod* and to Captain Ahab, and to the whale. But he does not know what it all means. He can witness and inform, but he cannot explain any more than Ahab can. To explain an obsession away adequately leaves the reader almost nothing to do.

It is often a mistake for a writer to give the narrative reins to an obsessive unless the novel is organized to produce a comic effect. You need an explainer, someone who will make a social effort in the direction of the reader.

Let's take another example of a novel that almost everybody knows, *The Great Gatsby*. It too displays a traffic jam of emotions. Here again we have the central character in the grip of an overriding fixed idea: Gatsby wants Daisy Buchanan, wants her obsessively. But what does Gatsby *really* want? In F. Scott Fitzgerald's consideration of the dynamics of nostalgia, Gatsby's rather like an adolescent who can't get a date with the most astonishingly beautiful girl in the class (such girls usually date guys like Tom Buchanan), and therefore Gatsby, or Gatz, vows to become somebody else, somebody rich and famous so that one day Daisy won't refuse him. He is ashamed of the person he is, the person who cannot have Daisy. Therefore he will become another person, The Great Gatsby.

That she will be a different Daisy does not seem to occur to him. Given this situation, Daisy, for Gatsby, is no longer a flesh-and-blood woman. She's become an overdetermined, congested, hyperfetishized object representing everything unspoken that he wants. He wants to rewrite and recapture the past. He wants innocence. He wants charm. He wants romance and enchantment. On top of all that, as a bootlegger, he also wants respectability. He's like a drug dealer who wants to be a Rotarian. He wants to be that contradictory thing, a genuine fake. There's hypocrisy in all this, but also a kind of innocent grandeur.

Once again, narratively, we have what I'd call the Ishmael-principle: Gatsby can't tell his story, so Nick Carraway does. And once again, innocent and not-so-innocent bystanders go down with the ship, or, in this case, the car. In Fitzgerald's novel, a woman is run over by a speeding automobile, the hero is shot to death in a swimming pool, and the end of the novel details a mess that no one wants to clean up. Nick Carraway leaves the geographical scene of the crime, though he is slower to leave its spiritual locale, and he still can't fully explain Gatsby's obsession. Part of him admires it. But Gatsby's obsession bleeds out into the whole American landscape, and after a while, he seems to be not just Jay Gatsby but a true red-white-and-blue American who has suffered, in a phrase from a Weldon Kees poem, a "ruinous nostalgia."

If Gatsby had somehow narrated *The Great Gatsby,* if he had survived his own story, we would be presented with a monotonous, unreliable, fixated landscape, but this hypothetical example is absurd anyway: Gatsby doesn't have the necessary distance on his own situation even to begin to narrate it.

Both Jay Gatsby and Captain Ahab are playing a strange and unauthorized version of *Careers.* Gatsby claims that he wants Daisy. That is, he wants love, but he really wants something else that he can only get by getting her. That "something else" in the form of his subterranean blues, reverberates long after the book is over. The power of fantasy in *Gatsby* is stronger than the reality that underpins it.

Similarly, Ahab wants to kill the white whale, but his reasons are both metaphysical and personal and so complex that readers are still trying to make sense of it. Ahab's ambitions are bigger than the white whale. The white whale is therefore a red herring. A writer doesn't need to make complete sense of the congested subtext to create a fine novel or a compelling story. Does size matter? *Moby-Dick* feels like an epic. Smaller obsessions seem more in keeping with our own time: Walker Percy's *The Moviegoer,* André Gide's *La Symphonie pastorale,* or Penelope Fitzgerald's *The Blue Flower* are about small obsessions that feel quite large, as is Nick Hornby's novel *High Fidelity,* which is about a certain variety of comic male obsessive behavior.

In any case, we have no critical language to talk about scale, about how to measure the size of the story.

In the kind of story in which the subtext has gone underground, the trouble arises from the character's having received exactly what he or she wanted for so long. This sort of story begins when the game of *Careers* is over, and you have won what you wanted. We might call this *the story of those wrecked by success.* Stories like this crucially depend on how they're staged.

Rainer Maria Rilke, in *The Notebooks of Malte Laurids Brigge,* invents a disease—a purely speculative disease—whose only identifying feature is that it takes on the characteristics of the person who has it. Although Rilke does not get down to cases, I think he means, or is talking about, people who are careful and who sicken and die of their carefulness; or others who are generous and gradually get poisoned with that; or anyone whose virtues walk through a mirror and come back as vices, looking the same, but dominant. Another word for this process is piety, in its negative sense. You get pious about what you believe in, and soon you become a grotesque embodiment of that belief, wrecked by success. You have gotten what you wanted, and you are ruined.

The phrase, "wrecked by success," is not mine, but Sigmund Freud's. Freud was of course primarily interested in what he regarded as the neurotic unhappiness that arose whenever you couldn't get what you wanted, when the housekeeping of the superego kept you from satisfying a basic desire. But toward the end of his life he was equally concerned with the neurotic unhappiness that arose when you got exactly what you *had* wanted. These are the stories of what would have happened after Ahab had killed the white whale and returned to New Bedford, and what would have happened after Gatsby won Daisy Buchanan and she moved in with him. Melville never wrote this kind of story, but Fitzgerald did, twice, in an early draft of *Gatsby,* and in *Tender Is the Night.*

In an essay from 1919, "On Those Wrecked by Success," Freud is unusually tentative: he argues that it is peculiarly difficult to know why unhappiness so often stems from a satisfaction of desires. But it happens all the time, and it creates mind-haunting narratives. Rather tellingly, he uses the play *Macbeth* and more particularly the example of Lady Macbeth as his central case study. He argues, in a very roundabout way, that Lady Macbeth's unhappiness after becoming queen arises out of a guilty conscience and that her sort of neurosis follows from the satisfaction of a desire that often involves guilt of an Oedipal sort. That is, when we get something we have wanted, in some private recesses of our minds we feel guilty about replacing our parents. The evidence Freud provides is interesting even if the explanation sounds wrong.

What if wishes and fantasies turn out in some cases to be more powerful than their real-life satisfactions? This is a mysterious feature of life that F. Scott Fitzgerald mulled over. In an early draft of *Gatsby*, which was then called *Trimalchio*, Daisy actually packs her bags, leaves her husband, and arrives at Gatsby's house, at which point Gatsby, of all things, *sends her away*. This seems both plausible and crazy. He's finally gotten what he wanted, and he refuses it. The flesh-and-blood woman, it seems, interferes with the fantasy of the very same woman. Fitzgerald did not save this scene, I think, because it was already implicit in his novel.

Hidden-story possibilities exist in the satisfaction of desires, of stories that *begin* when the explicit desires have been satisfied, and the congested subtext, full of rogue fantasy and obsession, starts to take over. Finality is just another illusory spot on the continuum. When the game seems to be over, the real game and the real story are actually just starting up. This is almost the entire subject of Willa Cather's hair-raising little novel,

My Mortal Enemy, about a woman who marries out of love, love only, nothing but love, and lives to regret her choice bitterly, and not because she doesn't get what she wants, but because she does get it, and that's all she gets.

Or think of John Cheever's story "The Swimmer." In this story, Neddy Merrill decides to swim home across the line of swimming pools stretching eight miles from the party he is attending to his house. But something happens in this story, something goes wrong. Along the way, the landscape shifts and gets degraded, and by the time Neddy gets home, he is weakened, and his house is mysteriously locked and rusty and empty. What has happened in this story? The subtext, it seems, has pushed its way into the foreground. As in many Cheever stories, the subtext seems to be concerned with what you get whenever impulses cannot be stopped and lead to prolonged impulsive behavior. Cheever's stories often are about actions that start out with an impulse that becomes repetitive—an impulse that turns into a sort of addiction of impulses that leads to the derailment of ordinary life and thus to desolation. All this can happen narratively in one day, as it does in "The Swimmer." The narrator tells us, "He had done what he wanted, he had swum the county, but he was so stupefied with exhaustion that his triumph seemed vague."

Vague, indeed. Get what you want, and you are ruined:

> The house was locked, and he thought that the
> stupid cook or the stupid maid must have locked the
> place up until he remembered that it had been some
> time since they had employed a maid or a cook. He
> shouted, pounded on the door, tried to force it with
> his shoulder, and then, looking in at the windows,
> saw that the place was empty.

Cheever's "The Swimmer" ends here, a landscape of radical unease. We are decisively beyond plot with these images, deep in a world configured by impulse and dream. William Maxwell, Cheever's editor at the *New Yorker,* once said in an interview that, as an editor, he could not follow Cheever into this realm. In lesser hands, the shift from realism to objectified subtext— the dreamworld of Neddy's broken home—might seem gimmicky. But Neddy has prepared our way to this vision by his foolishness, his alcoholism, his cheap romanticism, his anti-Semitism, and his mania.

Finally, we come to that grand master of congested subtexts, Franz Kafka. Kafka's novel *The Castle* is virtually all subtext. The symbolic and the virtual and the subtextual are so powerful in Kafka that they have pushed the literal reality virtually off the page. *The*

Castle is very clear about its symbolism, but rather unclear about its characters' precise actions. The reader can often guess at what the story means without being sure what the characters are actually doing.

I feel as if in talking about ironic twists and "be careful of what you wish for" stories, I am on the verge of what Walt Whitman calls "a usual mistake." I don't want to simplify what is actually intricate. When these complex psychological twists and turns are imagined as devices and employed mechanically, the stories that result can have all the subtlety of that long-running TV series, *The Millionaire*. Week after week, the nearly invisible John Beresford Tipton, like God, or some sort of Prime Mover, gave out a million dollars through his assistant, Mike Anthony, to some unsuspecting (well, who expects a million dollars to descend, like a flock of birds, from nowhere?) recipient. Week after week, within the half-hour span of narrative time, both viewers and characters were amazed to discover that a million dollars typically did not improve their lives. Often, a windfall turned out to be a catastrophe-in-disguise. Surprise! Once the viewer got beyond the premise—this is often true of TV—there was almost no show.

Those writers and dramatists who employ switcheroo plots, from Guy de Maupassant to O. Henry and Roald Dahl and Alfred Hitchcock in his television series, depend upon the expectation that the reader will not be able to guess what will be switched, or how. If there is an art to contrivance, it involves masking all forms of coincidence as free choice whose unfreedom remains in concealment. Therefore, the only conditions under which subterranean desires function in an interesting way in such stories are those that breathe a certain air—the air of freedom, of possibility, so that the artist's hand is well-disguised. If there is bait, before the switch, the bait should have a certain complexity.

Now that J. F. Powers's collected short stories have been republished, it is easier to claim that he is one of America's more subtle practitioners of the form. His dramatic irony is remarkably nonjudgmental. An ability to stand back from the scene without punishing his characters unduly gives his stories a strange comic pathos. Almost no other American writer has been able to manage this particular tone as well. Its formal difficulties may account for his small production, a lifetime total of three books.

Dramatic irony arises from a prank of fate. Sometimes this prank of fate is the result of a character's hypocrisy or ignorance, but often it is simply the connivances of chance. In either case, the character asks for one thing but gets something else that's completely unexpected. It's *Careers* when you ask for love and get a revelation instead. Characters can easily be shown up or humiliated by using this technique, but they may be illuminated when they're caught off guard and can't say what they mean.

As an example, I would like to refer to Anton Chekhov's often-cited "The Lady with the Dog." In this story, a counterpointed set of narrative branchings cause the main character, Gurov, to discover that what he thought he wanted is not in fact what he truly wants at all. The beauty of the story arises from what he has not asked for and had not known about.

Gurov begins the story as a middle-aged, slightly bored married man who imagines having a fling with the lady with the pet dog while on vacation in Yalta. He has that fling—that particular desire is satisfied fairly early on. But what causes the story to branch and grow is that Gurov appears to have fallen in love with Anna Sergeyevna. This love is incomprehensible to him, and it feels like a catastrophe. The object of his love is not extraordinarily pretty, and he himself is middle-aged, long past the time when emotions of this depth and complexity would (he thinks) logically have been sparked.

The love that Gurov begins to feel opens his inner life to a set of revelations he had never previously glimpsed and does not want. Nor does he become es-pecially articulate about what he feels. His feelings are out of proportion to his abilities or opportunities to describe them anyway. The story remains elegantly concise at the same time that the protagonist, Gurov, discovers that the most important features of life that you want to talk about cannot be spoken of in polite society. No one will listen to you, or you don't know how to say what you mean in a way that does honor to you, or the entire subject of what is in your heart is taboo. For the first time in his life Gurov has something to say, but no one to whom to say it.

An additional narrative irony is that Gurov discovers that, given the circumstances in which he has found it, love makes him miserable. It enlarges him as a human being, makes him conscious of his soul, and gives him an inner life, a feeling for textures and tones and emotions, but this mature love, as opposed to romantic love, does not lead to happiness. It feels like a punishment. At the end of his story Gurov has no idea of how to proceed. His complacency was unimportant, but his newfound unhappiness is hugely significant.

Idea for an interesting story: give the character exactly what s/he wants, and see what happens.

Flannery O'Connor, that great bard of savage dramatic reversals, deploys bait-and-switch tactics time after time, relentlessly, story after story, with grimly brilliant results. She punishes her characters for being stupid, hypocritical, or self-righteous and even punishes them for good intentions. Her stories particularly

despise do-gooders, those children of the Enlighten-
ment, who constitute her standard villain-class. The
Grandmother in "A Good Man Is Hard to Find" asks
for a car ride and gets the Misfit at the end of the road.
Julian, in "Everything That Rises Must Converge," tries
to show up his mother for her segregationist hypocrisy,
but gets shown up for his own spiritual pride and loses
his mother in the bargain. Sheppard, in "The Lame
Shall Enter First," is hideously punished by fate for
presuming to help the no-count Rufus Johnson. The
comeuppance that fate doles out to her characters is
painted in fun-house primary colors, and the violence
has a B-movie sadism to it. Tender mercies have no
place in these stories. Their thinly disguised disbelief
in happiness and their creative cruelty have a tendency
to shock first-time readers. She claimed in one of her
letters that people are often so obtuse about their own
lives that it sometimes takes a blow to the head to open
them up.

As a counterexample, J. F. Powers occupies an opposite corner from Flannery O'Connor: he rarely shows
up his characters for didactic purposes. His imagination is not nourished by cruelty, and he respects
human love, about which Flannery O'Connor knows
almost nothing. Powers uses dramatic irony in the
form of dramatic transference. The wounds are there,
but hard to see until we notice them in ourselves. He is

much more lenient with his characters than almost any other American writer with a satirical bent. He therefore takes a bit of getting used to, given the subdued comedy of his stories.

Powers had several subjects, but tended to concentrate on the worldly life of priests in the semi-rural Midwest. Powers himself lived most of his life in southwestern Minnesota, and a quality of Midwestern mildness, a sort of calm equanimity, is apparent in many of his stories. The spiritual lives of Powers's priests are invisible and unremarked-upon. The strategy is to present these men (and nuns, too, sometimes) as human beings who are struggling to get by from day to day almost without reference to the central inward fact of their lives, their faith. Catholicism in these stories is seen to be a vast, worldly arrangement of semi-comic domestic particulars. It is Catholicism without most of its beliefs on display and with no visible charm, a worldly setup that is run like a business. Powers ignores the usual markers of identity and instead pays attention to the markers of identity that no one else has bothered with.

Powers's form of stage-managing typically reverses the expected life stories of his priests. He unearths small scenes to illuminate the entire life and then presents the life in a paradoxical relationship to itself. In

"The Valiant Woman," for example, the entire story is played out in one evening at the rectory, beginning with three characters, Father Nulty, Father Firman, and his brave, strong, horrible housekeeper, Mrs. Stoner. No doubt Father Firman has gone into the priesthood for perfectly good reasons, but what he has ended up with, night after night, is a domestic life with Mrs. Stoner, who is a handful.

The day being Father Firmin's birthday, his friend Father Nulty has come over to help him celebrate. But the dinner has been, as the narration says, "a shambles," thanks to the housekeeper's relentless gossip and nagging. She gossips about the bishop, who has lost his appetite, she calls another rival housekeeper "a damned liar," and she is more interested in the business of the church—converts, particularly, and their reliability—than are the two priests. The priests are no longer particularly interested in Catholicism because it is their life, their vocation. Catholicism is Mrs. Stoner's avocation and her obsession, and she cannot get enough of it. She wants to talk about what she's read in *Reader's Digest*—the atom bomb and steering wheels made out of soybeans—while the two priests want to talk about their friendship and the intimacy they share, but Mrs. Stoner will not allow much of that. She is jealous.

She guards the house and Father Firmin, and she

has tenacity. The priests used to drink wine "or better" when they got together. Now they have been intimidated by Mrs. Stoner into drinking water. They have to rush through the meal, and they allow Mrs. Stoner to dictate the conversational topics (she sits at the table with them), and she manages to intrude to such a degree between the two old friends that Father Nulty quickly leaves after dessert, at only eight o'clock. Mrs. Stoner is domestic with a vengeance, and she and Father Firman are, in a sense that is not buried very far beneath the surface of the story, married to each other. Mrs. Stoner as a pseudo-wife takes up a lot of oxygen. As the story observes, "She hid his books, kept him from smoking, picked his friends (usually the pastors of her colleagues), bawled out people for calling after dark, had no humor, except at cards, and then it was grim, very grim, and she sat hatchet-faced every morning at Mass." But she *is* at Mass and sometimes the only one there. She is a saver: she "saved money, saved electricity, saved string, bags, sugar, saved—him. That's what she did. That's what she said she did, and she was right, in a way. In a way, she was usually right." Notice this: not a savior, but a saver.

This paragraph is the expository, as opposed to the dramatic, climax of "The Valiant Woman." The narrative makes it clear that the title is not meant ironically, or at least not completely. Mrs. Stoner has saved Father

Firman, and she continues to save him, but only in a way—that is, *her* way, rather than his. This is not about Catholicism; this is about a subtextual marriage and its grievous injustices. And like many dissatisfied spouses, Father Firman schemes about how to get rid of this woman, his nonwife, but cannot imagine himself carrying through on any of his schemes.

The game of *Careers* that is being played out in this story presents a lifelong marriage, punctuated with wry dramatic irony. What if you wanted a life of the spirit and ended up circumstantially married to Mrs. Stoner instead? What if you wanted to save your soul, but found that what was being saved was string and sugar, money and electricity? Mrs. Stoner is, as her name suggests, a rock, but upon this rock what church is being built? The domestic one. What Father Firman expected and asked for is not what he got, but he has to live with it. The result is a form of comedy, metaphysical comedy and the comedy of manners, subtle and difficult to write. The story concludes with three scenes. The first is of the nightly card game between Mrs. Stoner and Father Firman played with viciousness and ferocity as soon as Father Nulty has left. The game the priest and his housekeeper are engaged in night after night is honeymoon bridge.

Powers is meticulous in the staging of this card game. He begins with the way that Mrs. Stoner pushes the card table up against where Father Firman is sitting, the "leg of the card table sliding up against his leg,"—the physical world hitting the physical body, the crowding of the characters on their limited stage—and the way she shuffles the cards, "with the abandoned virtuosity of an old river-boat gambler." The first detail is one of pure physical intrusion and intimacy, the sort of tiny tangible detail that brings a scene to life. The second brings to the reader a metaphor that encapsulates Mrs. Stoner for the rest of the scene, in which she skunks Father Firman with a grand slam. "She was," the narrative tells us, "awful in victory. Here was the bitter end of their long day together, the final murderous hour in which all they wanted to say—all he wouldn't and all she couldn't—came out in the cards." This sentence signals the presence of a congested subtext in the story, an inability to be articulate, all that they wanted to say to each other and couldn't or wouldn't say making itself visible in the card-playing.

This is all comedy, it is true. But an alert reader would notice those words, "awful" "bitter" and "murderous." Both Mrs. Stoner and Father Firman feel something like rage: at their lives, at their domestic arrangements, at being paired with each other, rage at existence itself. The subject has flipped over and revealed its shadow-side. Comedy has momentarily disclosed its darker traces, its anchor pinnings, its desperation, the source of its weight. Murder lies at the heart of this domestic card game, that and vindictiveness.

After the game, Father Firman stays in his chair for a while, rocking, "the nightly trip to nowhere." In the next scene, in which the two of them go off to their separate bedrooms, we learn that Mrs. Stoner has given herself the guest bedroom rather than the back bedroom, the servant's quarters. We watch and listen as Father Firman allows himself to think the subtext of the story, that Mrs. Stoner has considered Father Firman a husband ever since the time when she first surfaced at the rectory. But this is the unthinkable thought—any thought considered unthinkable qualifies as a subtext—and it engenders in the story a series of exclamations, oaths, exclamation points, and negative assertions. "God! God save us! Had she got her wires crossed and mistaken him all these years for *that? That!* Him! Suffering God! No. That was going too far. That was getting morbid. No. He must not think of that again, ever. No."

Father Firman is the only human being within range who cannot think this thought. Every alert reader of the story has thought it, which is where the dramatic irony comes from, and all the other characters in the story, including Father Nulty, have thought it because it has been acted out in detail. Only Father Firman has not thought it because we are all obtuse about the self-contradictions that are closest to us and that we are most sensitive about. Father Firman is obtuse about this particular situation, so close to home that he is conveniently blind to it.

Although we live in a post-Freudian, post-humanist, postmodern, post-everything age, there are still plenty of unthinkable thoughts around, and in the Chekhov tradition they serve as the hard core of narratives. An unthinkable thought is not one that hasn't occurred to somebody, nor is it a thought that someone considers to be wrong. An unthinkable thought threatens a person's entire existence and is therefore subversive and consequently *can* be thought of and *has* been thought of, but has been pushed out of the mind's currency and subsumed into its margins where it festers. Dark nights of the soul are lit by inconceivable ideas. Any story may draw its source of power from an unthinkable thought.

Returning at last to the story's final scene and to Father Firman: as he goes to bed, he is pestered and tormented by a mosquito. He is naturally in a rage because he has dimly intuited that life has played a prank on him and paired him off permanently with Mrs. Stoner. Therefore, in his rage he rushes around his bedroom swatting at the mosquito and in his rage swings his weapon in the vicinity of the statue of St. Joseph, which he knocks over and breaks. This noise rouses Mrs. Stoner, who comes down to his bedroom to save him—she is, indeed, courageous and valiant—thinking that the noise was "burglars murdering you in your bed." Murder, again, in her imagination this time. When he says that it's a mosquito, and only the female bites, she corrects him: yes, only the female bites, but she needs the blood for her eggs. Mrs. Stoner knows such things, being a faithful reader of *Reader's Digest.* The story thus skims over what I would call a botched epiphany, but Father Firman has no time for it, and the story ends with him once again in rageful mid-lunge.

J. F. Powers likes to maneuver his characters into situations like this. They have been upbraided, but this is not Flannery O'Connor country. His characters do not typically hang themselves, rub quicklime into their eyeballs, or shoot anything that moves when they discover themselves living in a state of self-contradiction. Powers sees the condition of self-contradiction as common to humanity—and thus a wonderful source of stories. His small but beautifully detailed fictional territory shows the reader that no one ever quite wins at the game of *Careers,* not even priests, who are supposed to know the rules, and who are, in fact, the guardians of the rules. But fate does not particularly respect priests or anyone else, and this irony constitutes one of the wellsprings of narrative.

Unheard Melodies

In his senior year of high school, my son visited various colleges hidden away in small academic towns to see which one he might want to attend. These rituals are familiar for both parents and their college-age children, and bittersweet for everyone involved. All such scrutiny is a long prelude to a permanent parting. The pain can be reduced, however, by the colleges' willingness to allow idle parents and their anxious children to drop in on classes-in-progress. The parents may know nothing of the subject matter at hand, but out of a kind of institutional pity are permitted to sit in the broken plastic chairs in the back row and listen. One autumn afternoon, therefore, I found myself in a sunny philosophy seminar room in a cozy Midwestern college (my son was in another classroom), where the philosopher whose work was being studied happened to be Søren Kierkegaard. On that day the text at hand, *Philosophical Fragments,* was under discussion, and the topic of the day was the problem of how to think about the unknowable.

To think about the unknowable: at first this seems, well, absurd. But it isn't, or it isn't, *quite.* The students—

raffish, extremely bright, beautiful, brashly argumen-
tative, and eccentric—leaned back in their similarly
broken chairs, blew their noses, ruffled their long hair,
and made brilliant observations about Kierkegaard's
gnomic and anguished propositions. For me, the subject had a kind of gigantic significance. Everybody,
I thought, should be pondering this issue. How *do*
we think about the unknowable? *Can* we think about
it at all? Is it merely foolishness to try? Does it make
any sense to reason *from* what we do know *to* what we
don't know?

The question has an excellent pedigree and is one
of those adhesive pieces of philosophical flypaper to
which many generations of thinkers get stuck. In any
case, although I sat in that seminar room for a mere
hour, and have since gone back to Kierkegaard, I still
am not certain of his reasoning or his procedures, his
arguments *to* based on his reasoning *from.* But the
problem of the unknowable leads, at least for me, to an
adjacent related problem, very much of our time and
moment, a problem of great social importance: the
problem, that is, of how to think about the unheard.

In this I am not referring to overtones, or the half-
suggested, or the implied. Nor am I speaking about
God's speech to mortals, which, as Kierkegaard might
say, we may choose not to hear. We are no longer in

the territory—if we ever were—of John Keats's Grecian Urn. "Heard melodies are sweet, but those unheard/ Are sweeter . . . ." Well, sure, of course. But, no: in our time the unheard is unsweet. It is a form of blockage, distraction, drainage, noise control, private censoring, survivability, drugs, egomania, fuckyouedness, and sheer impatience, the result of the too-muchness of contemporary life Sample: "I don't have the time to listen to you, even if you're standing in front of me, right now, this very moment, talking. You can scream, and I will, like, *not* hear you." *My ears are sealed.*

Test question: when was the last time you were on an airplane and actually listened to the flight attendant as he instructed you in how to snap, and then how to unsnap, the seat-belt buckle?

Second test question: why has the word *"Duh,"* employed ironically, reappeared in common usage?

The survivor of ordinary American daily life has to develop good filtering mechanisms simply to get from one day to another. Keeping the toxic levels of daily sense information at a minimum is no easy task unless you are, say, Amish, or you have thrown away your TV set and your computer and don't get out often. Effective filtering is particularly difficult for anyone who lives in a major metropolis. Filtering may not be a uniquely modern phenomenon, but the sheer quantity of information, and its hyperaggressive marketing (elevating the nonessential into the critical, exemplified by the Fox News Alert), may be unique to our time. When I imagine my grandfather sitting in an airport-terminal waiting area underneath a television set broadcasting the Airport Channel, I imagine him losing his mind, the way lakeshore is lost through erosion. I cannot imagine this same grandfather (he died in 1921) in superhighway traffic and not also giving in to a panic attack. A form of madness now being theorized by social psychologists results from a crucial failure to block out sensory noise to a sustainable level. Overstimulation seems a syndrome shared by children and oldsters—such types don't know how to keep the hubbub away, at a safe distance, and often their reaction to it is to scream. Many commentaries have argued that attention deficit disorder is a by-product of the too-muchness of modern life. Its victims walk over the coals of contemporary stimulus and, for some reason, their feet get burned.

The word "distraction" has some etymological relation to "madness." But distraction, the mental state in which information cannot be separated from noise, is hardly the same mechanism as psychic deafness and referential denial. Deafness and denial manifest themselves when we can't stand to absorb what's being said. Narcissism and egomania and psychic vulnerability are the three great pillars of the Tower of Voluntary Deafness. They are the silent markers of subtexts in all dialogue; contemporary dialogue is marked by all three of them, and they are the signs, in good writing, of what Gertrude Stein once called the excitement of our contemporaneousness. If you're a good writer, these days, you pay attention to the way that people don't pay attention.

A woman who once said to me, "I'm not listening to you. I just turned off my hearing aid," had no hearing aid and was using a current expression of that particular year. The following year, the new expression was, "Talk to the hand." But even here, the energy of denial has to be separated from the cooler, glassier shield that narcissism erects to guard against the pain of others.

These days, the best and most artful dialogue is marked by the inattentiveness of its characters.

For the purposes of clarity, I am going to separate "the unheard" into two categories, with examples to follow. The first form of the unheard results from denial, an unmethodical way of not hearing dangerous or intolerable information. Some information, usually personal, is simply unbearable and goes unacknowledged. Our psychic systems cannot stand the strain of hearing it. The second form of the unheard is more complicated: it can result, first, from the kind of filtering we do daily, a manner of selective attention that in our time has become a survival procedure, and what is typically filtered is informational noise, or bullshit. We don't need to listen to what we don't need to hear. Advertising has taught us how not to listen at length, for hours; it has been the great progenitor of the sublime art of tuning out.

The second category of the unheard, a subset of it, radiates a peculiar, private blankness. Here I am concerned with what happens when important and even passionate information is conveyed, but drops down into the void of the listener's own indifference and inattentiveness. This is a particularly intriguing form of unhearing because its marker on the face of the non-listener is a glassy and unintelligible smile. Indifference-unhearing is not a form of denial, nor is it a form of everyday filtering. This kind of unhearing is, instead, a kind of psychic impermeability, a mode where nothing gets through—an unattended switchboard.

Within this mode, the pain of others becomes bothersome, an annoyance.

In second- and third-stage narcissism, nothing gets through that does not directly address oneself, but the self can only be addressed in certain ways—through corrosive wit, for example, an endless deflection, by means of a distracting style, of a genuine subject. The true narcissist, it seems to me, feels the pain of a perpetual wound. The wound is both peripheral and somehow central. This pain makes him or her distractable. But the wound, having no clear definition, is largely indescribable. Yet it seems to demand description, even though words are inadequate to it. (In some versions of the myth of Narcissus, Narcissus's scream is soundless.) Most of the narcissist's conversations therefore have a lengthy, free-floating, and often witty complaint built into them. One of the only forms of conversation that flames the true narcissist into attentiveness has to do with reparations. The narcissist is always waiting, in one stance or another, for the world to offer its apologies. If there are no apologies, then admiration will do.

I would like to provide a few instances of denial first because it is the clearest and most straightforward mode of unlistening. Also, it is quite simple to understand, like a huge systems breakdown on the receptor end of the radar. We know that in families, one way of handling psychically charged material is simply to leave it all unspoken. But what happens when a subtext is spoken, when it is uttered, and *it still goes unheard?* At great cost, what has been set in denial has risen to the surface and then sunk again because no one was able to see it or hear it. The receptor system has simply broken down under high-tension stress.

A chilling instance of this occurs midway in Tony Kushner's *Angels in America* in Part One, "Millennium

Approaches." Joe, the Mormon lawyer, married, a closeted gay man, finally gets around to calling his mother, Hannah, to tell her the truth about himself. The dialogue begins with some inquiries.

JOE: Mom, did Dad love me?

HANNAH: What?

JOE: Did he?

HANNAH: You ought to go home and call from there.

JOE: Answer.

HANNAH: Oh now really. This is maudlin. I don't like this conversation.

JOE: Yeah, well, it gets worse from here on.

(Pause.)

HANNAH: Joe?

JOE: Mom. Momma. I'm a homosexual, Momma.

Boy, did that come out awkward.

(Pause)

Hello? Hello?

I'm a homosexual.

(Pause)

Please, Momma. Say something.

HANNAH: You're old enough to understand that your father didn't love you without being ridiculous about it.

At this point, Hannah instructs Joe to go home and to get a good night's sleep. A harmless subject is substited for an inflammable one. This sort of thing happens in daily life all the time. "You're going to leave me? Wait! What do you think of this cheap domestic champagne?" Gay literature and much romantic literature generally is loaded with moments of unhearable truth of this variety, in which the unlistener is exposed in his or her obtuse obstinacy. (There is a very good example of it in William Trevor's story "Torridge.") Joe's confession is an obvious blank to Hannah, a nothing that is unheard and unnoted and punctuated by pauses. Quite capable of not hearing what she doesn't want to hear and can't process emotionally, she asks her son if he's been drinking (it's a sin) and then insists that he go to bed.

The American model for such dramatic moments, Eugene O'Neill's play *Long Day's Journey into Night,* is built out of two subtexts so painful for the characters to witness that their manifestations have become *almost* unseeable and *almost* undiscussable elephants-in-the-living-room—that is, Edmund's illness and Mary's drug addiction. Edmund's illness threatens his life, and Mary's addiction threatens her stability. O'Neill found the personal and autobiographical materials of this *Long Day's Journey* so intensely painful that he could not bear to see it—this, his own play; he stipulated that no performance was ever to be presented during his lifetime. He thus wrote a script that was, for him, literally unhearable. In some sense, as a playwright, he reproduced a situation that exists within the play he wrote.

The power of denial in the creation of theatrical dialogue and perhaps in creation itself is hard to overestimate. Denial battles desire every day, with denial usually given most of the cultural advantages, including the codes of politeness. Drama must correct the balance. Our blind spots, the sources of our denial, serve as resources if we can find them and strategically write around or through them. Writers have a tendency to go into an alias to write about the unwritable anyway; we become different people to write about our personal toxic materials.

For O'Neill, the situation in *Long Day's Journey* was unwritable and unseeable, and therefore had to be written, but in a kind of code. O'Neill's play is an example of a bad situation that gets worse, slowly but surely dragging other characters into it. Within a vortex, the author or some bystander needs to see clearly and transhistorically, even if the characters can't.

O'Neill's play would be static if there were not some counter-energy to all the denial going on in it. Denial alone constitutes only negative energy on which to build a story. It leads to dramatic immobility, a refusal to move in any direction, an insistence on "No."

A drama requires an opening of the wound. *Something* has to happen. In this respect, O'Neill was lucky in his choice of characters in *Long Day's Journey into Night,* since all four of the major characters are incessant self-dramatizers (what I would call "sparkplug characters"), and they are very bad listeners who listen, if they listen at all, selectively.

Self-dramatizers know that people are looking at them, but what they're not good at is paying attention to others. They command your attention by speechifying and turning spotlights in their direction, but they rarely listen carefully; they've lost the gift for it. Their actions are densely rhetorical, done to practiced turns. Having lost a sense of what the other person is saying, they often don't know what world they inhabit, which is why their emotions can explode unpredictably— this is what happens again and again to all four of the Tyrones. People like this are great characters to write about as long as the story or other characters notice how stagy they are.

This leads us into the second form of the unheard, the now-common procedures of filtering. If most conversation is going to consist of bullshit—even pleasant bullshit—one must remain in a state of heightened alertness for that moment when some statement of importance is actually going to be said. At times, the statement is so out-of-keeping with the rest of the discourse that the resulting rupture cannot be repaired. Sincerity always trumps bullshit, but only if somebody in the room is paying attention. The shock-of-sudden-attentiveness sometimes seems to me a peculiarly American moment, but I always have to correct myself: it isn't. British literature revels in sudden shifts in tone and heedfulness.

In the Comedy of Manners, no one is listening with much care until someone shows up who is naïve, sincere, or better at the game than anyone else, at which point everyone's game is endangered. In the nineteenth-century novel, a major character can suddenly reveal a flash of obtuseness or a failure of breeding and thus change the course of the story. Jane Austen's Emma surprises herself by half-consciously insulting a friend, for example, and it is a surprising moment because we learn that her shallowness includes malice. Breaches of tone—and a sudden focus on them—are so common in Jane Austen's novels that their plots tend to turn on their modulations, a tradition that is still quite alive in Evelyn Waugh's *Brideshead Revisited.*

The mode of conversation I am describing now as "filtering" is not art until some artist notices it. It is a "sort of" listening to people who are "sort of" talking. Most statements are therefore in a condition of approximate wording, and no great precision is necessary until the moment arrives when the conventions of the comedy of manners give way, and the central characters get up the nerve to say what they really mean. The noise that precedes this moment is what we now mean by blahblahblah or yaddayaddayadda. It is not quite blather, because if you listen carefully, heavy machinery is sometimes being moved behind it. The heavy machinery threatens to fall through the floor, breaking both the stage and the illusion of everything-is-all-right.

—I said to him, if you really believed what you wrote there, you'd be morally obliged to blow your brains out.

—Well, *whis*ky's all right, said the girl with the bandaged wrists,—but for God's sake don't give it gin, gin stunts the growth, we tried it on a kitten.

Nearer by, the woman in the collapsed maternity dress said, —Cross-eyed people bring me bad luck.

—Not just cross-eyed, the tall woman went on, —but with a withered hand, on crutches, and an idiot. Can you imagine *one* person having all those things? *And* in a suit with a pleated, belted back?

That was William Gaddis, a few lines from the behemothic party scene in *The Recognitions.* With these elements in view, we have entered the country later mapped out by Lorrie Moore.

Lorrie Moore's fiction has a scaffolding of wit that visibly gives way as her narratives progress. In her fiction, wit covers a kind of hilarity-spiked terror. Her first collection of stories, *Self-Help,* interestingly arrived on the scene at about the same time that academic studies in eighteenth- and nineteenth-century conduct manuals for women also began to attract attention. Lorrie Moore's stories seemed to lay out a series of rules for people catastrophically down on their luck, "How to Be the Other Woman," being the best-known. The stories were blissfully intelligent and often very funny, but at their core they seemed to turn American pragmatism against itself, as if to suggest that the long history of "self-help" in our culture is a maniacal misreading of the category of practicality. Even in a culture of pragmatism, no set of rules will work in conditions of extremity, especially when other people are listening selectively, or not listening at all. Metaphysical and spiritual pratfalls result, but by the time they do, no one is laughing. Her fiction thus presents desperate conditions in a disconcertingly lighthearted way. Reading her fiction, you notice time and again when a situation has stopped being funny, even as the characters try urgently to pretend that all remains comedic. The dancers go on dancing long after the orchestra has stopped, and the audience stares, aghast.

Her characters invariably arm themselves with attitude; and this self-arming marks her work as a form of comedy of manners. The narrational strategies of her fiction display a kind of brilliance that inevitably fails the characters who try to adopt them; this brilliance cannot alter their circumstances, but merely colors them in bright highlighted hues. Her fiction is quite straightforward about the way that urbane wit and hip worldliness, once useful as filtering mechanisms, collapse under pressure, a process especially noticeable in her story "People Like That Are the Only People Here." This subject gives her work its timeliness and its urgency and its weight. Her characters use wit to sustain themselves in conditions where wit ordinarily cannot be mobilized, and, in addition, *cannot be heard.* Like other great writers of social life, Lorrie Moore writes both about wit and about its deafened audience.

For example, in her story "You're Ugly, Too," the protagonist, Zoë, is at a costume party in New York City and has met a man, Earl, dressed as a woman. Zoë has been suffering from stabbing abdominal pains. "Actually," she tells Earl, "I have been going to a lot of doctors lately." After Earl asks what's wrong, Zoë says that she's had "mammograms. Next week I'm going in for a candygram." After looking at her "worriedly," Earl offers her two stuffed mushroom caps; Zoë jokes that it'll probably "be a gallbladder operation," whereupon Earl changes the subject to Zoë's sister's upcoming marriage.

The subject turns to love.

> *"Love?"* Hadn't they done this already? "I don't know." She chewed thoughtfully and swallowed. "All right. I'll tell you what I think about love. Here is a love story. This friend of mine—"
>
> "You've got something on your chin," said Earl, and he reached over to touch it.

Translation: Were you speaking? I hardly noticed. Zoë then proceeds to tell Earl a horrifying story about an award-winning violinist who moves to the Midwest, is humiliated by the indifference of her boyfriend, and finally commits suicide. Earl's response to this story is, "You're not at all like your sister." Translation: I didn't like your story and I wasn't listening and I'm not going to respond to it and now I'm changing the subject.

At this point in the story, all pretense of wit has collapsed—sexism, fear, and obliviousness in the form of filtering have done it in. Zoë, uncomically, asks Earl if the word "fag" means anything to him. Earl replies that he shouldn't go out with career women, and, following these logically placed non sequiturs, the story concludes with a muted, subtle, and quite disturbing act of violence, at which point no one is laughing, or should be.

When people are incapable of listening, when they are stone(d) deaf or blind to each other, the resulting condition may seem comic if the observer has the requisite distance, which observers in these circumstances seldom do. Comic dramatic writing depends, at least in part, on misunderstandings, mishearings, misinterpretations, misplacement, comic self-centeredness, and a daily diet of broken-off conversations. All this can be funny to watch and to listen to. But then, very quickly, it modulates into the peculiar hellish isolation of the person who faces a blank wall, in the form of a nonlistener, or a compulsive interruptor.

There should be a wise discussion somewhere of the nondiscourse of modern narcissism. We all know the type who generates it: after all, who has not heard hours and hours and hours of self-conversation by virtuosi of the boarded-up self? Such people are almost incapable of conversation except when priming their own pumps. In perpetual therapy administered to themselves by themselves, they must be roused to conversation by a question about their biographies, like opera singers waiting for their cue. Once incited, their arias have commenced and cannot be stopped until the curtain falls. There are no questions directed at the listener, no inquiries about subjects of common interest, no curiosity about larger subjects, no real diversions, no points of interest *out there.* Certainly there can be no conversational back-and-forth. How could there be? There are only statements, followed by other statements, leading eventually to overstatements, when the listener eventually tires, flags, sighs, grows tried of saying, "You're right," and turns away.

One of the occasional diversions of *Seinfeld* or of *Sex in the City* was to notice how often the characters failed to listen to anyone else. The scripts for these shows consisted of parallel-play monologues disguised as dialogue.

Once, years ago, listening to an acquaintance then on the staff of an English Department, I tried to stop the onrush of monologic verbiage rising incrementally, overstatement by overstatement—*this person was stupid, that person was an idiot, this critic was as dumb as a box of rocks*—by saying that a parade was going by outside my window, and I had to go see it. We were on the phone. My acquaintance paused, said, "Seen it now?" and continued as before. Another friend of mine remarked about this person: "He's like a monster who wants you to play with his toys."

Another way of thinking about what often passes for conversation takes us toward my central subject—the half-noticed and the half-heard. Such gaps between lines of dialogue can open up the subterranean, given the way that pieces of sequential dialogue simply refuse to match up. Conversational slippage comprises the non sequiturs of everyday life. Therapists are always on the lookout for such forms of unlogic. Sometimes, what you don't hear tells me more about you than what you actually say. Our times are marked by mishearing and miscueing and selective listening and selective response—features associated with information glut and self-inflammation. Distraction may be a symptom of attention deficit, a characteristic feature of our data-soaked era, or it may simply be an outgrowth of simple hypertrophied egomania. Everyone knows someone who listens in a hypothetical manner.

In the house on Noe Street, Big Gene was crooning into the telephone.

"Geerat, Geeroot. Neexat, Nixoot."

He hung up and patted a tattoo atop the receiver, sounding the cymbal beat by forcing air through his molars.

"That's how the Dutch people talk," he told Alison. "Keroot. Badoot. Krackeroot."

"Who was it?"

He lay back on the corduroy cushions and vigorously scratched himself. A smile spread across his face and he wiggled with pleasure, his eyelids fluttering.

"Some no-nut fool. Easy tool. Uncool."

He lay still with his mouth open, waiting for rhyming characterizations to emerge.

"Was it for me?"

When he looked at her, his eyes were filled with tears. He shook his head sadly to indicate that her questions were obviated by his sublime indifference.

That is from Robert Stone's "Aquarius Obscured," and it contains that glassy smile of indifference I mentioned earlier. Such dialogue resists its own meanings (such dialogue is functionally empty) by serving as an indicator of whether the characters are paying any attention at all, and, if so, to what.

Dialogue plays the chords of its own cultural moment. In the era of multitasking, people probably talk more and listen less than they ever did. Talk *is* cheap and has been for some time, but now it has become recreational (I am thinking of cell-phone mania) in a way that listening has not. Close listening now seems almost freakish, or naïve. Only shrinks practice it, and for money. I recently re-read Thomas Hardy's *Tess of the D'Urbervilles* to see if there is ever an occasion in that novel where Hardy's characters don't listen. (Here I am making a distinction between not-listening and misunderstanding.) No. Although the characters do occasionally misunderstand, they are always listening to each other very carefully. The novel's silences are quite eloquent.

In our own time, entire novels have been written about nonlistening, selective listening, and parallel monologues, particularly the novels of Ivy Compton-Burnett and Henry Green, in England, and those of William Gaddis, in America. Examples of extended nonlistening would quickly grow monstrous and unbearable (qualities that Gaddis flirts with, as the moth flirts with the flame). These writers point to ironic displacements of subject matter, the conversation of the perpetual deferral. It's here, then it's gone. The subject matter of a conversation within a scene, apparently comprehensible, gradually goes off the track into nullity. Gaddis is the epic novelist of the null set. His characters start in a fog and stay there. In book after book his subject is always capitalism's tendency to turn information into noise and art into garbage. His novels are brave, mostly failed attempts to recycle the noise and garbage back into art.

Distractedness compounds the inability to keep your mind on one subject with protracted uneloquence, the inability to say what you mean. The peculiar feature of distraction is its colossal dramatic potential. But if some subjects are undiscussable, some actions may also become invisible or unseeable; that is, there are some actions that are sometimes so painful to watch that we cannot watch them. When a subtext breaks out in action, a caul of invisibility may still surround it.

The drama of the willfully invisible event happens most often in families or tightly knit social groups where appearances are being kept up. Claustrophobic "togetherness" is the breeding ground of theater, from *Long Day's Journey* to *Angels in America* and *True West.* What playwrights understand is the dramatic power of obtuseness and how to get it on a stage. They understand how much wit it takes to keep up appearances.

In Paula Fox's *The Widow's Children,* Peter Rice, an editor of books, arrives at the office of Eugenio Maldonada to inform him that Eugenio's mother has died the night before. The Maldonadas, all of them, as presented in this novel, are monsters of a sort: underparented as children, they are now in a state of perpetual self-regarding semi-obliviousness. Eugenio is a travel agent who lives in his office, and when Peter finds him, after closing time, Eugenio is sewing on a button to his suit. Following Peter's announcement of Eugenio's mother's death, Eugenio "was still, his eyes half closed. Then he picked up the jacket and pulled the needle through." He asks Peter whether he'd like some instant coffee or tea. He asks about his sister and brother-in-law, and their imminent departure for Europe. He asks about their travel agent.

> "... Do you know my sister never *mentioned* this trip of theirs to me? I didn't even know they were leaving the country." He drew his thread through the fabric, then bit it off with his teeth.
>
> "My mother always warned me not to bite thread," he said. "She thought it was very bad for teeth. Did you know my mother?"
>
> ... [Peter] was confounded by Eugenio's reception of the news. He didn't know what to do with Eugenio's digressions. After so many years, the Maldonada perversity still took him by surprise, forced him to admit the precariousness of custom. These people had not signed *any* social contract.

Exactly right. And the part of the social contract that many of our contemporaries have refused to sign is the part about paying attention. Is Eugenio self-absorbed, or unable to react to the news of his mother's death, or indifferent to it? It's not clear. *The Widow's Children* is a book with so many subtexts that they become cancerous—the past is eating away at the present to such a degree that the present, in effect, dies and disappears. Characters live so completely in the past that whatever gets said to them in present time is filed away and responded to retroactively—that is, once it becomes another manifestation of something that has turned historical. This is an aftermath novel; the dreadful has already happened, so what anyone says to anyone else in present time is filed away, as if for some kind of timed release.

It may seem strange to say so, but the great fallacy of most written dialogue in fiction of our time is that all the characters are listening. But everyone knows that we have grown into a nation of nonlisteners. What gives the writing of Eugene O'Neill, Tony Kushner, Lorrie Moore, Paula Fox, and William Gaddis its particular distinction is the notice it has taken of what people do not notice. In truly wonderful writing, the author pays close attention to inattentiveness, in all its forms.

In fiction, the forms of evasion are every bit as interesting, conversationally, as truth telling.

It's fascinating to find yourself in the company of someone who is preoccupied and dazed, simultaneously. Some time ago I was involved in a conversation with a woman who had broken up with her boyfriend. She patiently described his faults to me, his essential faults, and then the secondary faults, the ones she was willing to overlook, and when I offered some noises of sympathy, she patiently described his faults, the same ones, all over again, the primary and the secondary, as if I hadn't heard her litany the first time. And then I realized that what I was witnessing might be more complicated than absentmindedness: she was in such pain that she wasn't listening to herself. Unable to monitor her own monologues, she couldn't remember what she had already said. Her thoughts were so earsplitting that she probably thought they were spoken aloud even when they weren't. Meanwhile, her speech had become somehow silent to herself.

If people aren't paying attention to each other or even to themselves, well then, we have to pay attention to that.

Inflection and the Breath of Life

"It isn't what you say; it's *how* you say it." Emphasis on the "how." This pronouncement from my high school speech class is worth considering whenever a sur- face conversation seems to be blandly innocent while the depths roil with demons. *How* you say something is more likely to get you in trouble than *what* you say. When, following the assassination attempt on Ronald Reagan, the then Secretary of State, Alexander Haig, held a press conference and said he was in charge, his trembling voice inadvertently let the American people know that he wasn't even in charge of himself.

Suggestions about the inner life, and the soul's se- cret preoccupations, arrive by means of overtones. Pandemonium can be struck with one clear if barely audible note.

Before Steven Spielberg, and before *Jurassic Park,* and before *The Lost World* was found and filmed and sold to millions, before all this, there was, and still is, along Highway 12 in southern Michigan close to the Ohio border, a humble tourist trap, Dinosaur World. A little roadside attraction in Michigan's so-called Irish Hills, it shares the neighborhood with a Mystery Spot, where the laws of gravity are violated and where, the billboards claim, scientists are baffled; a fireworks outlet called The Boom Box; the Dwight D. Eisenhower Presidential railroad car next to a stand selling chocolate fudge; Chilly Willy's putt-putt golf course; and other odds and ends of local tourist interest, including a water slide and a go-cart track. Most of the businesses could use a few coats of paint. The place has seen better times.

When our son was seven years old, my wife and I decided to make a day of it and take him to Dinosaur World. We figured he was ready for the terrors of prehistoric killer raptors and reptiles. He thought so, too.

Outside Dinosaur World, a fountain of sorts spouts water tinted dark blue, thanks to heavy doses of dye. You pay the entry fee and are loaded onto a train of what seem to be about eight rusting golf carts, Cushman Cars, linked together. There are no rails. These carts are on kid-sized rubber wheels. While you wait for the guide, you watch the Triceratops, the one dinosaur available for free viewing, constructed out of chicken wire and some sort of painted plaster. His mouth opens and shuts every five seconds, like an elf in a department-store Christmas-window display. The sound of reptilian indigestion emerges from a hidden loudspeaker.

At last our guide arrived. He was a high school

kid. This was his summer job. August: you could tell from the expression on his face that he was exasperated and bored. He looked at us, his customers and fellow adventurers, with ferociously undisguised teenaged indifference. "Welcome to Dinosaur World," he said in a flat monotone. "We are about to go into a land that existed before time began." He had spoken the line so often that it had turned into one word. "Weareabouttogointoalandthatexistedbeforetimebegan." He plunked himself down into the driver's seat of the head golf cart and began speaking into a microphone, aided by feedback. "Fasten your seat belts," he said, unnecessarily. "Lemmeknowifthereareanyquestions."

The hapless train, moving backwards in time in several respects, followed the asphalt road around the displays of chicken wire and painted plaster. The multinational technology of Disney World was far away. Every so often the guide would stop to explain a prehistoric wonder, reciting his script with ill-concealed indifference. At the climax of the tour, close by an eight-foot-high killer dinosaur, he mumbled, "This is the fearsome Tyrannosaurus Rex." Then he yawned, and the three of us, my wife and son and I, burst out laughing. The guide looked slightly taken aback. "What'sa matter?" he asked. "You're not scared?"

I shrugged. I thought of Leo Tolstoy's remark after reading a play by the writer Leonid Andreyev. Tolstoy had not been impressed. "He puts on a sheet and says, 'Boo!'" Tolstoy said, "but I am not afraid."

Samuel Taylor Coleridge's "willing suspension of disbelief" is an unstable category. What makes it curious is not the "suspension" but the "willing." None of us at Dinosaur World expected to believe what we were seeing. We expected to be invited to a little party where the host acted as if *he* believed in his own flimflam and was inviting us into that *as if.* The tour guide had an actor's job to perform a role. His responsibility was to encourage us to suspend our disbelief. That was his task, his summer job. To pretend within certain limits that he was inside a moment of time and that we could join him there, he had to hypnotize us a little by means of his act. This projection of belief is the technical problem of narratives concerning fantasy materials. Pretending to be interested, he had to convince. When you cry, "Wolf!" you have to sound as if you mean it. Otherwise, no wolf. As Orson Welles once said, there are no magicians, there are only actors who are playing magicians. A great magician is a great actor. And great actors perform hypnosis on a small scale and cause us to fall asleep into another world.

Any reader becomes involved in a story when an attachment forms to a set of narrated events, or when the tone of the narrative has so many signs of emphasis that it rouses itself to life, and disbelief is suspended. The story starts to enact itself, often by means of inflection. When someone cries "Wolf!" believably, that conviction spreads outward. A broken, twisted face appears before you, speaking: "Once a bitch always a bitch, what I say. I says you're lucky if her playing out of school is all that worries you." (William Faulkner, *The Sound and the Fury*) You can't hear these lines properly without hearing the malice dripping off of words.

Inflection, which I am defining here as the tone with which the wording is conveyed, particularly when applied to extreme events or circumstances, can elevate fiction into sudden shocking life. It signals belief and urgency. The urgency wakes us up. At such moments, emotion is not recollected in tranquillity but is reenacted before our eyes. The story is singing or groaning itself awake. And yet another world is awakening, too, the one I have been referring to as being "beyond plot." Inflection is the sign of spoken intensity, conscious and unconscious: an inflection offers a glimpse of what is usually unseen. If you say something the wrong way, your subterranean realm is suddenly revealed. Tonality takes you from what has literally been said down there, to the realm of shadowy implications.

Writers of fiction not only stage events, but often suggest how those events and statements are to be inflected; that is, how they are to be acted, pitched, and voiced. Fiction writers thus serve as both the creators and the directors of their own work. My dictionary defines "inflection" as an alteration in tone or pitch of the voice. This might seem to be a small matter, but an alteration in tone or pitch can be the difference between being inside a moment and being out of it, or between fighting words and a statement of love, using the identical phrase, such as "You're really something," a completely meaningless statement without a tone or context to support it.

A monotone equals monotony. In the Land of Dullness, everybody speaks like a robot and goes about their mechanical business with their heads down. They eat their words, sentence by sentence. By contrast, inflection gives us both an indication of life-in-the-moment and a sense of how a phrase is to be understood. It constitutes the difference between a tonal deadness and a sense of urgency conveyed through shifts in tone. Shifts in tone alter the meaning, from sincerity to irony or exasperation to incredulity. Given sufficient urgency, our disbelief is suspended. When someone grabs you by the lapels, you tend to listen to what he says.

Every page is silent until the reader's imagination revives it, adding tonal shifts, exclamation points, underlinings, over- and undertones. Without salt, the rice is tasteless.

In critical confrontations statements are inflected when the words alone won't carry the required emotional meanings. Teenagers are capable of transforming themselves from bored affectless speakers to drama queens in seconds. "So, they're *sitting* there, and I'm, like, doing *the tour?*" It's like saying: I'm overinvested in what I'm telling you! I can't help it, listen to me, this is a fucking emergency! For the inarticulate, sheer feeling substitutes for eloquence. In the perpetual crisis of adolescence, who cares about poor or approximate word choices? Every sentence is an emergency, and emergency sentences acquire their voltage through high-pressure emphasis.

Of course, this state of affairs has, in literary work, its mirror-vice: overinflection, the particular deadening rat-a-tat-tat of prose that has gone purple from hyperemphasis. There is an odd kind of monotony to writing and speaking of this kind. The effect has some resemblance to an incessant television commercial. When inflection is applied everywhere, without limit, we are back in a kind of robotized verbal-delivery system. The novels of James Ellroy sometimes strike me this way, as hyperinflected tonal artifacts in which the first quality to be misplaced is a feeling for what should be emphasized, and where, and how. His landscapes lack all perspective and proportion. Everyone is crying "Wolf!" all the time. Perhaps that is the point.

All the varieties of inflection are particularly necessary to those who don't have access to official language and official eloquence—to teenagers, the dispossessed, minority groups, and the baffled and broken, the hopeless and downcast, the obsessed and the fantasists, the inarticulate, outsiders of every kind and stripe, and those who are feeling two contradictory emotions at the same time, particularly if one emotion is unofficial. The official emotion goes into the statement; the unofficial one (which exists at the subtextual level) goes into the inflection. Incidental stress is the tonal outpost of fugitive feelings and of layered or compounded emotion. As the eloquent music of idiomatic language, it is the homing device of effective liars, magicians, outcasts, losers, and poets.

Is some fiction underacted? Is such a critical category even imaginable? Stories can be told without being brought entirely to life, and one of the signs of this semi-lifelessness, this zombie condition, this Dinosaur-World narration, is that the whole story seems undervoiced, as if we had gone into a bad dream of the 1950s, and the writer had not quite believed his own story, or was an agnostic about it, or didn't want to get involved in it, or was bored, or wanted to keep a safe distance from it or from the audience. The story stays calm. And everyone is allowed to fall asleep.

It is our business to wake everyone up. By force, if necessary.

I am on an Amtrak train in Oregon. Behind me a little girl is commenting on the trip, town by town, mile by mile. When we cross a river, and the bridge under the tracks is not visible underneath us, the girl says to her mother, "I'm frightened! We'll all fall into the river. We will be *destiny*." But the little girl is being ironic. I immediately write down the sentence and am simultaneously plunged into despair about how to convey on a page the way the girl sang out the word "destiny."

Months later, the girl's misuse of the word "destiny" doesn't interest me so much as the joy that the little girl conveyed in role-playing a little girl who is frightened. She had mastered her own emotions by acting them out theatrically, for her mother. Her lack of fright— the subtext being her joy—projected itself distinctly through her happy inflection.

Given sufficient urgency, an electrical charge can be applied tonally anywhere, to any words. The art of acting applied to the art of writing provides a tonality for a line, so that we know how a totally meaningless statement like "You're really something" is to be understood, as a caress or an insult. For operatively vague statements, inflection fills in what the vagueness leaves

out. Good acting often gives us an unexpected color-
ation to a phrase, a reversal of what's expected, that
makes a scene with dialogue heat up without warning.

Much of what gets said in the course of a day comes
out strangely. We accompany our seemingly bland
statements with a large inventory of pauses, facial gestures, body movements that can intensify or contradict
the apparent meaning of what we're saying. "Pass the
rivets" is one thing, but "I love you" is another and requires a tone to support it. A person can say, "I love
you," while at the same time using body language to
disprove it. Conversations can go on entirely by means
of body language, as in dancing or lovemaking.

The plot of Francis Ford Coppola's remarkable film
The Conversation hinges entirely on how a single line
of dialogue spoken by two young people is inflected,
and how the movie's protagonist, Harry Caul, hears
it or mishears it. The line is "He'd kill us if he had the
chance." If the inflection, the emphasis, is on "kill," then
the two people who are overheard in the conversation
are frightened for their own safety ("He'd *kill* us if he
had the chance"). If the emphasis is on "us", then they
are plotting a murder themselves ("He'd kill *us,* if he
had the chance," i.e., we have to get to him first). In the
second reading, by the way, it helps to have a pause,
a comma, after "us." In that particular reading of the

line, the single emphasis flips the statement's apparent meaning onto its back.

Stage actors sometimes describe a "flip" as an unexpected reading of a line that wakes you up, shocks you into awareness. The actor reverses the emotion in a line reading so that the expected tone gives way to an unanticipated tonal shading buried contextually, and an urgency—an immediacy—results. Suddenly a subtext appears, arising from an emotional emergency. Christopher Walken has described seeing Laurence Olivier playing Dr. Astrov in Anton Chekhov's *Uncle Vanya* and being taken aback when Olivier reversed the usual tone of Astrov's first long speech. Near the beginning of Act One, Dr. Astrov comes on the stage and describes losing a patient, a railroad worker, who has died on the operating table under chloroform. Most actors deliver this declaration in a tone of slightly depressive unhappiness, reflecting Dr. Astrov's despair over his inability to do much good for his patients.

But that was not the inflection that Olivier used, according to Walken. Olivier *laughed* during this speech, despairing alcoholic laughter. Exhausted and giddy, Olivier's Astrov suffered from a spiritual fatigue so intense that only broken laughter projected it. Watching Olivier laugh like that onstage was mesmerizing,

Walken reported: the "wrong" tone produced, not in-congruity, but a kind of hysterical sincerity.

One of the filmed versions of Vanya, *Vanya on 42nd Street,* has several moments of this sort, examples of a sudden drop into an emotional chasm by means of unexpected tone shifts. In the middle of Act Two, for example, when Sonya, among other inquiries, asks her stepmother, Yelena, if she's happy, and Yelena simply says, "No," both Julianne Moore and Brooke Smith play the scene with barely suppressed expectancy and giggles, as if they had finally been able to get to the questions they had always wanted to ask each other and were pleased with themselves for having done it. Unsolemn about these solemn questions, they feel girl-ish (the effort to get to be direct has worn them out), trading secrets back and forth while the men are out of the room. They can't quite shed the feeling of being co-conspirators, and they are shy, finding themselves—at last—emotionally naked.

Similarly, Wallace Shawn, playing Vanya, does so as if Vanya himself were doubled: Vanya feels despair about his own life, but in addition, he finds his own de-spair comic. Vanya is a desperate comedian, handling his despair through clowning. Shawn delivers the com-edy lines with a woebegone mournfulness and the lines of resignation with a strange, heady exhilaration, as if he were a brave heroic explorer, a sort of Scott-of-the-Antarctic, in the poorly mapped continent of patient despondency.

In Katherine Anne Porter's story "The Leaning Tower," set in Berlin in 1931, Charles, an American, has been staying at a hotel and then finds an apartment house where he would rather reside. His German isn't as good as he would like it to be, so, like most foreigners, he has to study facial expressions and body language to make sure that he has understood what he thinks he has heard.

In signing a lease for the apartment, Charles accidentally knocks over a little plaster Leaning Tower of Pisa in the landlady's parlor. The landlady tells him, "'It cannot be replaced,'" and then the author adds that the line has been said with "a severe, stricken dignity." Notice the compounded emotion, a sign that Charles is paying attention to her intonation. It is also an indication of how she is reinforcing her distress by theatricalizing it. We can see her physically stiffening, accompanied by a touch of phoniness. A few moments later, the landlady adds, "'It is not your fault, but mine. . . . I should never have left it here for—'" She doesn't finish the sentence. The text tells us, "She stopped short, and walked away carrying the paper in her two cupped hands. For barbarians, for outlandish crude persons who have no respect for precious things, her face and voice said all too clearly."

The landlady is playing to the gallery. Katherine Anne Porter signals here that conversations are far from over when people stop speaking, but continue in the burnt electrical silences that follow, often by means of facial expressions and body language. The most emphatic point in the sentence may arrive not with the last word but with a refusal to say a word, allowing the accusatory silence to hang there.

In the following scene, Charles goes back to his Berlin hotel to move his belongings and to check out. Here he must deal with the "sallow wornout looking hotel proprietess" and her "middle-aged, podgy partner." Charles had previously agreed to stay in the hotel for a month, but now, after eight days, he is leaving. What follows is a masterful scene of telegraphed malevolence and dramatized malice, indicated by both words and physical indicators. The characters are playing themselves but are also, enthusiastically, overplaying for their own pleasure.

"'But our charges here are most reasonable,'" the proprietess says, "her dry mouth working over her long teeth." This is an odd detail. In my first reading of the story, it stopped me cold. Excellent result: it is there, perhaps, to slow down the scene, and to convey the woman's anxiety and suppressed rage. But we also have those "long teeth" over which the mouth is working. She is chewing over something. She is wolfish.

"'You will find you cannot change your mind for nothing,'" she continues, in what we are told is a "severe, lecturing tone." We might figure out this tone for ourselves, but the statement of it intensifies the feeling and adds an aura of danger, a sense of the woman's inflexibility. She has a pedantic vehemence, like a violence-prone professor. Now the narrator illustrates the woman's facial change. "She glanced up and over his shoulder, and Charles saw her face change again to a hard boldness, she raised her voice sharply and said with insolence, 'You will pay your bill as I present it or I shall call the police.'"

Enter the proprietess's podgy partner, who, hands in pockets, smiles "with a peculiarly malignant smile on his wide lipless mouth." The author here is not only writing the words of the scene, she is directing them for us. We have faces and inflections. Charles pays the proprietess all the money she has demanded, to the last pfennig, and then the podgy man, whose "pale little eyes behind their puffy lids were piggish with malice," asks to see Charles's identification papers. This is an extreme situation, Weimar Germany, and Charles is on his guard, watchful for the signs of malice aimed in his direction. He means to survive in this poisonous locale.

Insisting on seeing the papers, the podgy man is then described through micro-details. "He seemed struggling with some hidden excitement. His neck swelled and flushed, he closed his mouth until it was a mere slit across his face, and rocked slightly on his toes." After Charles has shown him the papers, the man says, "'You may go now,' with the insulting condescension of a petty official dismissing a subordinate." In the next sentence, we learn, "They continued to look at him in a hateful silence, with their faces almost comically distorted in an effort to convey the full depths of their malice." Notice how the silence is being drawn out, and how this silence is not peaceful, but hateful. The silence vibrates with its own negative energy. Finally, after Charles has left the hotel under their "fixed stare," he hears, "as the door closed behind him" the two of them laughing "together like a pair of hyenas, with deliberate loudness, to make certain he should hear them."

The malice is marked by all its small details of gesture, speech, and hoaxing gratuitous meanness. But cruelty, as Henry James and Katherine Anne Porter knew, is increased and intensified by shades of detail. Cruelty lives off small signs and hints, closed rather than open doors. Subtle cruelty creates a web meant to catch the unwary, who are punished by small but incremental wounds.

Another tactic for combatting the zombie effect appears in Eudora Welty's "A Visit of Charity." The ground situation in this story is quite straightforward: Marian, a junior high Campfire Girl, has been assigned to take a flower to a retirement home for old ladies and to sit there and chat for a while. This visit of charity is part of the procedure for Marian's earning of a Merit Badge.

This ground situation is not particularly promising. The elderly have become commonplace pathos-targets, especially when they are afflicted with illnesses. Retirement homes and assisted-care facilities provide ready-made settings for literary opportunists.

But what Eudora Welty does in this story is to upset the expected tone of the story so that pathos is a minor element. Instead, there is a kind of scorched wit at work, not pitiless but in the service of genuine but very dark compassion and understanding, and this dry comedy moves the proceedings in the direction of what I will call for the sake of brevity the abyss. Suddenly, the mystery of existence opens up in front of Marian and the reader. Welty does all this by carefully inflecting every moment of the scene. After a few pages, Marian's old ladies stop being pitiful creatures, old Southern ladies down on their luck, and seem more like Beckett's tramps, Vladimir and Estragon, in *Waiting for Godot,* struggling with time and the absurd.

The reader is given, moment by moment, careful close direction detailing the scene. This *is* a scene and is not summarized; it has to happen in front of you. Marian has walked into the room with her gift of a potted plant. Two old ladies inhabit the room, one lying down and one standing up. The standing one has a "terrible, square smile . . . stamped on her bony face." I like that: a *terrible,* square smile. We're not told what makes it terrible. Nor are we told exactly how to visualize it. It seems contradictory. Her hand, "quick as a bird claw," grabs at Marian's cap. The room is dark and dank, and Marian starts to think of the old ladies as robbers and the room as the robbers' cave.

"'Did you come to be our little girl for a while?' the first robber asked." The plant is snatched out of Marian's hand. "'Flowers!' screamed the old woman. She stood holding the pot in an undecided way. 'Pretty flowers,' she added."

Did you come to be our little girl for a while? This is comedy, but the furies are writing it.

"Then the old woman in bed cleared her throat and spoke. 'They are not pretty,' she said, still without looking around, but very distinctly." After the first old woman repeats that the flowers are pretty, the old woman who is lying down says in return, batting the ball back in this peculiar verbal tennis game, that the flowers are "stinkweeds." Somewhat disarmingly, the old woman in bed is described as having a "bunchy white forehead and red eyes like a sheep." When she asks Marian, "Who are you?" the line is interrupted by dashes to indicate slowness of speech, and the author tells us that the words rise like fog in her throat and that the words are "bleated."

We learn that the woman in bed is named "Addie." Addie and her unnamed old companion then argue about a previous visitor and whether they had enjoyed that visit. Triangulated by the two ladies, Marian, the Campfire Girl, a frightened intelligent child, begins, very mildly, to hallucinate, to go off into the hallucinations of ordinary life created by the scene before her. At this point, Addie and the other old lady have a surrealistic discussion about who is sick and who is not and who did what as a child. The standing woman speaks in an "intimate, menacing voice," another unusual combination. This is interrupted by Addie's first long speech directed toward both her roommate and, I think, obliquely to Marian. The author gets out of the way here and lets the speech speak for itself.

> "Hush!" said the sick woman. "You never went to school. You never came and you never went. You never were anywhere—only here. You never were

born! You don't know anything. Your head is empty, your heart and hands and your old black purse are all empty, even that little old box that you brought with you you brought empty— you showed it to me. And yet you talk, talk, talk, talk, talk all the time until I think I'm losing my mind! Who are you? You're a stranger—a perfect stranger! Don't you know you're a stranger? Is it possible that they have actually done a thing like this to anyone—sent them in a stranger to talk, and rock, and tell away her whole long rigmarole? Do they seriously suppose that I'll be able to keep it up, day in, day out, night in, night out, living in the same room with a terrible old woman— forever?"

At the end of this speech, the author notes that Addie turns her eyes toward Marian, eyes that have gone bright. "This old woman," the author notes, "was looking at her with despair and calculation in her face." We then get an image of her false teeth and tan gums.

"'Come here, I want to tell you something,' she whispered. "'Come here!'"

Marian is frightened, we're told, and her heart nearly stops beating for a moment. Then Addie's companion says, "'Now, now, Addie. . . . That's not polite.'"

This scene, packed with seemingly contradictory emotions, throws into a blender Marian's fascination and terror, Addie's despair and calculation, her companion's fake sentimentality and cynicism—the scene is a mixture of despairing comedy, pathos, terror, and metaphysical giddiness. These elements are built into Addie's speech through the repetitive use of words like "empty," "talk," and "stranger," and the use of carefully deployed dashes and pauses. And they are then cemented by the brilliant tag following the speech, noting that Addie is now turning toward Marian with despair *and* calculation on her face. Addie is not feeling one thing. She is feeling several emotions at once. One of them makes her pitiable, the other makes her dangerous. We then learn that today happens to be Addie's birthday.

As if this weren't enough, when Marian leaves, the nameless woman (the other half of this terrible octogenarian tragicomic vaudeville team) who has been playing the straight woman to Addie's riffs of calculation and despair, this nameless woman then goes into a riff of her own. "In an affected, high-pitched whine she cried, 'Oh, little girl, have you a penny to spare for a poor old woman that's not got anything of her own? We don't have a thing in the world—not a penny for candy—not a thing! Little girl, just a nickel—a penny—'"

The "affected, high-pitched whine" notation tells us that this woman may have fallen into a moment of senile dementia. Or, more likely, she may be playing a role for her own amusement to scare and disconcert Marian, or maybe to get some money out of her. Like the woman in Katherine Anne Porter's scene, Welty's old woman is theatricalizing her own situation and speech. But no reader, I suspect, can be sure exactly what the tone is, and our uncertainty parallels the uncertainty that Marian must feel. You can see clearly and distinctly what you see, but you simply can't be sure of what you're looking at.

The scene presents these women, as Samuel Beckett does his tramps, with all the complicity of art, of realism flying off into the metaphysical and then flying back. The scene's feeling-tone can't be described in one word. What's going on is too overdetermined for that.

Much can be said for the uses to which the opposite— an uninflected voice—may be employed. Zombie voicings in literature may well echo our current conditions, particularly the bureaucratic ones, better than the hot-to-the-touch effects of inflection. There is something about uninflectedness that suits trauma, and data fatigue, and anonymity, very well.

What can be bothersome about uninflectedness from the last two decades generally, however, is that it can seem like a decadent form of hipsterism, a retro form of cool, of being removed, which can harden into

a posture. Against middle-class fake sincerity, fake pa-
triotism, and fake fervor of every sort, uninflectedness
and ironic withdrawal, at least since the 1980s, have
been deployed massively and effectively in every form
of postmodern art. It is now completely mainstream
and has been put to some interesting uses. George
Saunders, for one, is a master of the zombie tone.

> At Sea Oak there's no sea and no oak, just a hun-
> dred subsidized apartments and a rear view of FedEx.
> Min and Jade are feeding their babies while watch-
> ing *How My Child Died Violently*. Min's my sister.
> Jade's our cousin. *How My Child Died Violently* is
> hosted by Matt Merton, a six-foot-five blond who's
> always giving parents shoulder rubs and telling them
> they've been sainted by pain. Today's show features
> a ten-year-old who killed a five-year-old for refus-
> ing to join his gang. The ten-year-old strangled the
> five-year-old with a jump rope, filled his mouth with
> baseball cards, then locked himself in the bathroom
> and wouldn't come out until his parents agreed to
> take him to FunTimeZone, where he confessed, then
> dove screaming into a mesh cage full of plastic balls.
> ("Sea Oak").

Well, the people of the village *do* understand by
now. The miracle of Saunders's fiction is that the

zombie-dazedness of the beaten-down acquires, some-how (this is the miracle) a crazy eloquence, a back-from-the-dead intensity.

The guide at Dinosaur World was at pains to demonstrate that he was above what he was saying, detached from it, *better* than it. And so he was. But as triumphs go, this is a very minor one, and in its way is as much a miscalculation as overacting would be.

In his recent memoir, *Crabcakes,* James Alan McPherson describes a moment during which he listens to two African Americans flirting with each other. Then he remarks:

> The kindly flirtation between the two of them reminds me of something familiar that I have almost forgotten. It seems to be something shadowy, about language being secondary to the way it is used. The forgotten thing is about the nuances of sounds that only employ words as ballast for the flight of pitch and intonation. It is the pitch, and the intonation, that carries *meaning.* I had forgotten this.

Everyone forgets it. Nabokov once said that the price of being a writer was sleepless nights. But, Nabokov added slyly, if the writer doesn't have sleepless nights, how can he hope to cause sleepless nights in anyone else? If the writer doesn't indicate interest in the story through inflection, how can she expect the reader to be interested and willingly suspend disbelief? To close the book or finish the poem and to say, "You're really *something*"? And the something turns out to be *something*, after all.

Creating a Scene

Proposition A: In fiction we want to have characters create scenes that in life we would, in all likelihood, avoid. This contrasting attraction-and-avoidance turns out to be a terrible spiritual problem for young writers. In daily life, a writer may practice conflict-avoidance, but in fiction a writer must welcome conflict and walk straight into it. The writer may be aided in creating a narrative by having a repellant character around in the story, who in some significant way has lost control and who gets the entire narrative engine up and running.

Proposition B: When writers avoid conflict in an effort to keep up an appearance of control and placidity, they have confused the realms of life and of fiction: it is as if they are claiming that dramatic conflict has an element of vulgarity and that life, even as it is lived in fiction, is best conducted through a series of avoidance procedures. Such a course of action betrays a feeling of shame about the inner life and the sorts of resonance that the inner life can create in fiction—a shame that has not been successfully overcome, as it must be—spiritually and dramatically.

Some years ago, a friend of mine told me the story of how she came to be married. When I had first known her, she had been dating a rather quiet, undemonstrative graduate student in political science, a somewhat shy though physically rather large man and certainly aggressive whenever he played touch football, which he did on weekends, returning dirtied and bruised from his outings. This man's character had an attractive mix of qualities, she thought, both nurturing and fierce, and after a few months of seeing him socially she thought she was in love with him. She herself was a graduate student in biology.

After several months, this boyfriend had suggested that they go out to dinner in one of the more expensive restaurants in Baltimore. When he picked her up at her apartment—they were not yet living together—he was wearing a threadbare coat and tie. A small and almost invisible food stain discolored the tie near the knot, but instead of being dismayed, my friend was charmed by her boyfriend's inattentiveness to appearances, and in any case she was used to it.

At dinner, in the waterfront restaurant where he had made the reservation, she had ordered scallops when she noticed that her boyfriend was blushing. "You're blushing," she said. "How come?"

"There's something I have to do," he told her. The restaurant, which had a good local reputation, was rather crowded and noisy. As if she hadn't heard him, he re-peated, more loudly, "There's something I have to do." It seemed that he was working up his courage. He reached into his pocket and drew out a little box and opened it. In it was an engagement ring. Then he pulled back his chair and got down on one knee beside her.

"M——," he asked, "will you marry me?"

My friend remembers this moment and likes to tell this story not because she was pleased by the proposal, but because everyone in the restaurant was looking at them. She was embarrassed and amused by her own embarrassment. She examined the engagement ring and the stain on his tie. What she remembers saying in response was, "Yes, I'll marry you, if you'll please stop making a scene."

If you were raised in the genteel tradition, as I was, you avoid scenes, even when people say they love you. This is not the best preparation in the world for writing stories.

I live in a part of Minneapolis where several bookstores vie for my attention. One of them, an independent bookstore, has a fine selection of Native American lit-erature, fiction and nonfiction, and wisdom literature shelved close to philosophy. In the gigantic Barnes and Noble two miles away in the strip mall, by contrast, you can find large selections of almost every printed book that could be considered mainstream, including a large selection on writing. The books on writing, that is, books on the craft of writing, are shelved next to the self-help books, which have a section all to themselves. After you look at these selections for a minute or two, you start to notice that the books in the two sections have been commingling. Some of the writing books include pep talks, and some of the self-help books include the activity of writing as a means of self-improvement.

It's doubtful whether a lifetime's dedication to the writing of fiction has cured anyone of anything. Keats noted that writers spend most of their time trying to figure out if they're the healer or the patient. But as it happens, among these self-help writing books is one by a woman I happened to know when I was in my teens and early twenties, Brenda Ueland. At that time, thirty years ago, Brenda was in her eighties. She encouraged me, as she encouraged many others, to follow their particular ambitions. She urged me to be a writer, since I had claimed I wanted to be one. "'Better to kill a babe in its cradle than to nurse unacted desires,'" Brenda used to say, quoting William Blake. When she was in her eighties, no one could still match Brenda's fearlessness. Someone I knew said, "Brenda is always picking people up." I think this phrase was meant in both senses. She encouraged everyone to do what they wanted to do

THE ART OF SUBTEXT   119

and to do it sooner rather than later. Her book on the craft of writing is called *If You Want to Write,* and it consists of a series of pep talks, and in my local Barnes and Noble, this book is shelved under self-help.

In a materialist society, to devote oneself to non-material ends requires quite a bit of energy and resolve, and Brenda Ueland knew all about the difficulties in finding such resources, with the result that her book is a kind of exclamatory spirit-lifter. *If You Want to Write* is actually full of good sense about writing and life because Brenda Ueland could see through the hypocrisy of gentility quickly and easily. In one chapter, she wrote she had two rules she followed absolutely: to tell the truth, and not to do anything she didn't want to do. This is sensible advice if you have never been poor or unemployed.

If You Want to Write is aimed at the sort of person who wants to break out of the spiritual doldrums into the practice of an art and who has to get free of smug middle-class values to do it. Such a person needs strength of will to face up to failure and interrogations from practical-minded friends, who, in an effort to appear concerned, will ask, "How will you make any money?" or "How will you raise your children?"

In the short term, writing may indeed do some of the work of self-improvement and therapy, particularly for those who have been forced to confront what has been done to them and what they themselves have done to others. For all those who are working with people in prisons and in halfway houses and various shelters and affinity groups, I say, "Good luck and blessings on you," without ever doubting that literature and therapy are two different enterprises, and that their outcomes may be at war with each other.

The particular dark reflecting pool that literature presents to us quite possibly has no purpose at all, any more than great music does. The pointlessness of art is not an argument against it. It is simply a proposition that pragmatists worry over. Consequently, as a way to stave off pointlessness and the specter of a profitless activity, we—Americans particularly—tend to moralize and pragmatize the practice of literature. We sometimes try to avoid in our own writing and reading what we may find troubling in our lives. But what is good when encountered in life is often not good for literature, and the reverse: what's good for fiction is not always good when instrumentalized in life.

The distorting effect of wishes in the writing of fiction can hardly be overestimated. In fiction the force of a wish can result in the formal characteristics of fantasy writing. The story becomes the stage, not for truth, but self-actualization. We try to imagine the person as we would like ourselves to be and as a result write a banal and lifelessly idealistic story. Stories of this type commit a number of sins against literature, among them, first, the distortion of events in the service of a positive self-image, and, second, the habit of making people out to be better than they actually are.

In fiction we want to have characters create scenes that in real life we would typically avoid. Writers might want to have happy lives, but they fear the revenge of the genteel community if their writings are too lively. If they do, they give up their writerly badge of honor. Stories often require sparkplug characters—radically unpleasant types—as focusing agents. The refusal of a story to grant a wish, its refusal to be polite, genteel, or *useful,* offers manifold opportunities for the messy self-reproaches and grotesqueries characteristic of fiction.

The household of my childhood was one of prolonged silences. My stepfather was a learned, witty, irascible man who, as the years passed, enthusiastically developed a curmudgeon side. Every time he saw a highway under construction, for example, he called it a make-work project meant to keep the riffraff employed. He was also affronted by the slow speed limits posted near elementary schools. My mother, by contrast, had a strong will, but a Protestant and Midwestern middle-class reluctance to display it directly. When I had the nerve to give way to the angers of that house, particularly in adolescence, my mother would upbraid me by saying, "Now, Charlie, don't make a scene."

Where I came from, making a scene was considered vulgar. The lower classes created scenes: they shouted at each other and threw dishes and plates. Their lack of control indicated clearly why they should not be put in charge of things. We were certainly not supposed to follow their model. Whenever my stepfather saw a drama on television or in the movies in which people raised their voices in passion or anger, he would say, "Life isn't like that." He meant that people like us were not like that, or at least we weren't supposed to be like that, and above all we weren't supposed to create scenes of that sort. We were supposed to button it up, whatever "it" was, as a sign of our habitation in the professional-managerial classes. And the lives we led were the definition of what "life" was. What other definition could there be?

We ourselves were not supposed to be dramatic. Drama was for others, or for the purposes of entertainment. Along with being told not to create scenes, I was told not to tattle on people, which was worded as, "Charlie, don't tell tales." It is interesting to me now how the construction of a narrative—any narrative—was frowned upon in that household.

All this suppression was a product of my stepfather's latent Anglophilia and his ideas about self-control. Foreign customs and habits were all right in their place far across the Atlantic, where you had to have a passport to witness them, but when imported to America, these strange bohemian behaviors, beliefs, and their associated food groups—Catholicism! confessionals! pasta!—were merely comical.

But of course our family did create scenes, eventually. We shouted and misbehaved just as they did everywhere else. In order to recognize my own anger for what it was, I had to struggle through the layered insulations of our family's mock-gentility, just as I had to struggle through that same gentility to get at any passions I could claim as my own. Everything I had ever been taught as a child about self-control stood against every instinct that I eventually acknowledged or acquired as a writer of dramatic narrative.

What I had to learn—the lesson of bad behavior—was to honor the most profound desires I had, no matter how unpresentable or unsavory they might be, and to do it by creating scenes, on paper. First I created scenes in life, and then I put them into stories.

One curiosity of writers' workshops is that, when confronted with a highly dramatic scene in which the writer has probably gone for broke in the presentation of a crucial conflict, the workshop participants will habitually call the result "melodramatic." This is a way of saying that drama makes them uneasy and that the characters who create scenes are often unpleasant and unlikable. (It is of course true that freshman write fiction full of hideously overdramatized conflict, but they get over it once they try to become respectable and obtain jobs.) Overt anger and straightforward conflicts still strike many genteel readers as unrefined. There is nothing more vulgar than a fistfight in the country club.

A particular telltale sign of this discomfort is that in writing workshops certain kinds of characterizations often evoked and praised—those of Anton Chekhov, Leo Tolstoy, Alice Munro, for example—stand in contrast to certain other kinds of characterizations rarely cited, including many of those to be found in Fyodor Dostoyevsky. Dostoyevsky's greatness is famously difficult to describe. Dostoyevsky's most memorable characters are comically grotesque: sociopathic, demonic, and inconsolable, and the techniques he used to characterize them are probably unteachable. Chekhov, speaking for many, thought Dostoyevsky was self-indulgent.

Dostoyevsky's work is an ongoing problem for many readers and most graduate writing programs. Dostoyevsky himself had few winning qualities, and his most disagreeable characters can produce in the reader a feeling of nearly intolerable uneasiness that cannot be rationalized away. I mean this as praise. One of his translators, David Magarshack, has said that Dostoyevsky's political ideas cannot be taken seriously, and politics is only the half of it. Nor can Dostoyevsky's fiction be reduced to sensible or simple lessons about craft or style or even ethics—in some fundamental way, he is beyond all that.

An immediately recognizable feature of Dostoyevsky's characters happens to be their temperamental compulsion to create large-scale scenes. Like the drunk Marmeladov in *Crime and Punishment,* they are always grabbing someone by the lapel and breathing hotly into that person's face, asking for a word or two that may turn into a deranged monologue that lasts for the rest of the chapter or beyond. There is a collapse of narrative distance in Dostoyevsky, what the film critic and scriptwriter George Toles calls in another context "story distance"—a longitudinal perspective on events that allows us to judge those events disinterestedly. This collapse of distance gives the reader the frequent impression that scenes in Dostoyevsky's fiction are happening in some kind of dramatic location so close to you that you can't remove yourself from the scene. Reading Dostoyevsky is like sitting in the front row of a theater, where the actors' spit lands on your face.

Often Dostoyevsky's scenes have the quality of being both overcompressed with information and ragtag in shape, with a quasi-operatic dramatic intensity set at the highest possible limit, triple *forte,* close to frenzy. The scenes created in this manner boil over hellishly and comically. Everyone's composure breaks down or melts in the general heat. Climaxes are achieved before their proper buildup, and characters are regularly too voluble, or, at crucial moments, too inarticulate. Words fail them. Eloquence betrays them or hits the ear-piercingly wrong note. One never has the impression that *le mot juste* in the right context will solve everything. Instead of articulation, there is frenzied, superheated speechifying. Both heaven and earth somehow become implicated—humanity alone seems incapable of setting events of this colossal magnitude into motion—with the result that the human soul, the central player in these cosmic dramas, becomes as palpable as a kitchen knife.

Antagonists in Dostoyevsky are characterized first and foremost by their bad manners and by the outward manifestations of their inability to control themselves and to keep their souls in check; only secondarily are they made up of the flesh. If you are looking for the soul, watch for bad manners, which are definitive. Narrative events and personal behaviors in these novels achieve such high magnification that they *feel* cosmic even when the devil is safely offstage. The instability of his characters (Stavrogin in *The Demons,* Raskolnikov in *Crime and Punishment,* and Smerdyakov in *The*

Brothers Karamazov, among many others) is such that they cannot carry on normal conversations or behaviors even when their lives might depend on their ability to do so; besides, they have no interest in the everyday. Furthermore, they are without charm, and their wit—if they have any—tends to be without humor and takes the form of sniveling meanness or brutal sarcasm.

Dostoyevsky's characters have no access to the genteel habits of polite society. What politeness they may have melts away in the tumult of their moods, which invariably turn into passions. They lack usable charm. The whole point of pathology in Dostoyevsky's novels has to do with its colossal size and unassimilable nature. In this respect only, it resembles holiness. These characters are generously if not articulately rude, an offense in the eye of the reader and society, and they would be dismissible if the news that they bring—psychological, spiritual, political—weren't so important to the outcome of human society. They are the John the Baptists of wayward intellect and obsessive pathology, operating in the lower depths where the sleepless deformed brilliant intelligence is busily at work hatching plots that will change the course of history for the rest of us.

If a reader wanted to discover in literature the sources and mechanics of terrorism, for example, the sense of exclusion and mania and what Friedrich Nietzsche calls *ressentiment,* few authors would be as helpful in the endeavor as Dostoyevsky. He might well be the world's foremost psychologist on the rage of the outsider whose good ideas go psychopathologically out of alignment. He is the expert on the man who throws stones with no particular target in mind, the starving man who sets fire to the bakery.

Ongoing readerly discomfort with the Dostoyevskian protagonist is an endlessly renewable resource. In my experience it is almost never absent in the later novels. If the balance between demons and angels cannot find its proper pivot point, the size of the frame around the materials is also, always, deferred. How does one put these events in perspective? The very absence of perspective often appears to be exactly the point, particularly in *The Devils* and *The Brothers Karamazov,* and it was an issue that caused Dostoyevsky himself some problems in his final novel, in his efforts to refute Ivan's barren rationalism.

The Dostoyevskian protagonist is often busy creating scenes. By "creating scenes" I am describing not a technique in writing but a form of behavior. The first definition of scene creation is the almost ritualistic inability to follow the conventions of good manners. If good manners comprise the code of behavior that renders our behavior acceptable and thus almost invisible in polite society, bad manners make us visible, for good or ill. We become a spectacle. Bad manners put us on a stage, and a stage, as every writer knows, is what is required for dramatic force.

This leads to my second way of thinking about creating scenes: we create a scene when we forcibly illustrate our need to be visible to others, often in the service of a wish or a demand that we seek to impose. Creating a scene is thus the *staging of a desire.* No wonder genteel people fear scenes, even those that involve getting down on one knee, in a restaurant.

When I ask for another cup of coffee, I am not necessarily creating a scene, but if I get up on the counter in the diner and shout at the waitress and the chef that I must have my coffee, I am indeed creating a scene. I have become unpleasant and seemingly crazy. I am staging the drama of my mania. I have become slightly Dostoyevskian.

In writing textbooks a scene is usually defined as a completed action occurring within a unified time period in one place, the form of showing that is contrasted to telling. But creating a scene can also be the staging of a desire, making a darkness visible and dramatic. Such writing is unafraid of passion and of confrontation. It does not practice conflict-avoidance, but instead faces down conflict and follows its consequences to whatever end point may be required to resolve it. It may be as simple as a repetition. The woman in "Hills Like White

Elephants" creates a scene by saying, "Will you please please please please please stop talking."

We need to see what is at stake here and why dramatic writing is so often at odds with self-help. To import conflict-avoidance into fiction is to confuse realms, of what might work ethically in life versus what works dramatically in fiction. Fiction, a dramatic medium, asks writers to unlearn the habits of conflict-avoidance for the sake of revelation.

People who have practiced good manners and conflict-avoidance all their lives have to remember to leave those habits of mind at the door when they enter the theater of fiction. Stories thrive on bad behavior, bad manners, confrontations, and unpalatable characters who by wish or compulsion make their desires visible by creating scenes. Imagine Dostoyevsky's contempt at the idea that his characters ought to be more pleasant, more presentable. The perennial Dostoyevskian question is, "Do you want the truth or agreeable-seeming falsehoods?" Fiction is that place where human beings do not have to be better than they really are, where characters can and should confront each other, where they must create scenes, where desire *will* have its day, where all truth is beautiful. Fiction is the antidote to the conduct manual.

We are rewarded when we put on paper a convincing, enraged, articulate, plausible human being who is compelled to make a scene in front of everybody, or nobody. Of course all fiction does not require such characters. But they often serve as accelerants to set fire to everyone else. William Trevor's stories, for example, usually begin with an ultra-civilized British milieu, into which Trevor typically introduces a near-maniac. The maniac serves as the focusing agent.

In John Cheever's story "The Five Forty-Eight," the central character, a businessman named Blake, has had a brief affair with his secretary, the appropriately named Miss Dent. When the affair is over, he sees to it that Miss Dent is fired. Blake is a completely loathsome suburbanite who keeps up the appearance of gentility in business and at home, but whose inner life is hypocritical and self-deluded. In fact, as the story tells us, keeping up appearances is one of his hobbies—he criticizes another man, one of his neighbors, for his "long and dirty hair" and his corduroy jacket. But this dreary philanderer has no dramatic force until the late afternoon on a particular day when Miss Dent sits down unexpectedly next to him on the commuter train going back to Blake's suburb, Shady Hill, and announces that she has a gun pointed at him.

Miss Dent is a lunatic of sorts, but in Cheever's story she is a messenger of fate, and her lunacy is placed in a neutral dramatic space. As the character who creates a scene, she is the axe to open the frozen sea of Blake's soul. She can't help but act out her mania. She makes desperate accusations and by doing so gives the story a sense of urgency. With her gun pointed at him, Blake's time has run out, and Miss Dent has become his focusing agent. His world, or what remains of it, is about to acquire the value it has for anyone who is under an immediate threat of death.

> "Oh, [she says] I've been planning this for weeks. It's all I've had to think about. I won't harm you if you'll let me talk. I've been thinking about devils. I mean, if there are devils in the world, if there are people in the world who represent evil, is it our duty to exterminate them? I know that you always prey on weak people. I can tell. . . ."

This is Dostoyevskian, on a greatly reduced suburban American scale. All that Blake, a war veteran, can think about at first is what the bullet would do to him: ". . . it would rip out of his back a place as big as a soccer ball." But there's a hole in him already, Cheever suggests, a hole where his heart should be. When this unhappy couple arrive at Shady Hill, after Blake has come to think of the commuter train car as a "dismal classroom," Miss Dent orders him out. They walk to a coalyard. Then she tells him to stop. Here she begins to rave, a little, but her ravings make the emotional sense that Blake's reasonable meanness lacks.

> ". . . I'm afraid to go out in the daylight. . . . I only feel like myself when it begins to get dark. But still and all I'm better than you. I still have good dreams sometimes. I dream about picnics and heaven and the brotherhood of man, and about castles in the moonlight and a river with willow trees all along the edge of it and foreign cities, and after all I know more about love than you."

She makes him grovel—literally—and after she has done so, she can say, "'Now I feel better.'" She recognizes ". . . some kindness, some saneness in me that I can find and use. . . ." As for Blake, "He got to his feet and picked up his hat from the ground where it had fallen and walked home."

Most readers fall into Cheever's little trap. The reader's sympathy moves away from a seemingly normal man and becomes attached to a visionary bedlamite. But then, the visionary bedlamite happens to own the truth; the mania is, in effect, a means to an end. "'. . . Sometimes it seems to me that if I were good and loving and sane . . . if I were all these things and young and beautiful, too, and if I called to show you the right way, you wouldn't heed me. . . . ,'" she says. She is right.

Youth and beauty will rarely persuade anyone. She needs firepower to be convincing. She needs to create a scene. Sometimes what the classroom requires is a gun in the hands of the teacher, a point also made by the Misfit, in Flannery O'Connor's "A Good Man Is Hard to Find," and Belle Starr, in Richard Bausch's "The Man Who Knew Belle Starr."

A final example, from a book—Edward P. Jones's *Lost in the City* (1992)—that provides some of the most scrupulously observed scenes of urban life to be found anywhere in recent American fiction.

The book's subject is the African American population of Washington, D.C., and its ways of marking and recouping its losses. The stories' understanding of their characters owes as much to a Kafkaesque sensibility as to one schooled in the traditions of urban realism. The book's patient details are both hyperrealistic and dreamlike, dreams reported with slow-motion clarity and logic. Even the worst characters in the book understand the dream-condition of their lives.

> There was something in the air, but he could not make out what it was. He walked out of the park. He kept looking behind him, expecting something or someone, but he was alone on the street and he saw nothing but the swirling of dead leaves. He contin-

ued looking behind him as he made his way up 17th
Street. He took out the address book, but found he
could not read the names or the numbers under the
feeble street lights. . . . He did not know what was in
the air. ("Young Lions")

As dreams do, the stories often dramatize the effort to find a direction. A girl learns the geography of
the city by watching for her pet pigeons, emulating
their sense of position. A father whose daughter van-
ishes after he slaps her subsequently searches for her
by taking her school photograph around to the neigh-
borhoods he's never known, knocking at strange doors
and asking for her. The search eventually becomes all-
consuming (I am relying here on a beautiful reading of
Jones's stories by a former student, Andrew Cohen), a
search during which he glimpses the lives of strangers,
discovers a city, and ultimately redeems himself.

The book contains its own embedded metaphor
for the kind of dramatic micro-detailing it employs—a
model train set. It is, in effect, a model for the kind of
representation we will find in these stories.

In that world, there were no simple plastic figures
waving beside the tracks. Rather, it was populated
with such people as a hand-carved woman of wood,
in a floppy hat and gardener's outfit of real cloth, a

woman who had nearly microscopic beads of sweat
on her brow as she knelt down with concentration in
her flower garden; several inches away, hand-carved
schoolchildren romped about in the playground. One
group of children was playing tag, and on one boy's
face was absolute surprise as he was being tagged
by a girl whose cheek was lightly smudged with dirt.
A foot or so away, in a small field, two hand-carved
farmers of wood were arguing, one with his finger
in the other's face and the other with his fist heading
toward the chest of the first.

Detail-work of this sort sets up a permanent barrier
to stereotyping. Anyone described with such precision
must be a singularity.

Because so many of the book's characters feel lost,
or in *possession* of a loss, or have misplaced some essential part of their lives, they are required by the circumstances they have fallen into to make scenes, as if
only in this manner can they become visible to themselves again. Making a scene locates them on an emotional map. The stories—again, like dreams—sometimes
meander on their way to discovering what the participants' true feelings actually are; when everything is a
byway, there are no wrong turns. As one of my students once observed, these stories lose themselves in

a process akin to that of melancholia as Freud defined it, a mourning with no object, or at least a mourning radically ambivalent and confused about what it's grieving for.

If characters are capable of creating scenes, the narrative itself is then free to wander.

Take the grimly brilliant story "The Night Rhonda Ferguson Was Killed." The title announces a death, but of a character we don't see until the third page, and then only briefly. Our attention is caught by the title, only to have its sensationalism dismissed. The story's actual protagonist, Cassandra Lewis, is first viewed as she sits on a low brick wall outside her high school, smoking cigarettes and considering how she will punch out her teacher for having made an offensive remark. Cassandra's nickname is "Tank," and she is heavily armored with verbal obscenities and physical violence. In due course she leaves the wall and the pursuit of revenge and returns to her car, which she has borrowed from her brother-in-law without permission. Here she runs into the title character, Rhonda, a singer who is off to sign a record contract, and who the reader assumes will be the center of the story and of a murder. But Rhonda soon disappears offstage, leaving Cassandra listening to the radio in the car and smoking until two girls appear and propose an errand, which involves a monetary reward. Cassandra agrees to this errand because she has nothing else to do.

At this point the reader, wondering how Rhonda is going to be murdered, the suspense having been raised only to be withdrawn, might also wonder what Cassandra's random movements have to do with the death announced in the title. The relationship between the events is obscure until the errand is completed (significantly, a tableau associated with a divorce), and the girls drive over to a party one of them has heard about, whereupon Cassandra's borrowed car sputters and stalls. A young attractive man, Wesley, appears on the scene to help fix the car, and Cassandra is clearly drawn to him. Perhaps a love story is in progress. But as the young man, Wesley, begins to flirt with Cassandra, one of Cassandra's friends, Melanie, emerges from the house crying, her blouse torn. Another young man follows Melanie out of the house, claiming it, whatever "it" was, was all a misunderstanding.

An erotic adventure out on the street is thus doubled and made consequential by an erotic misadventure inside the house.

At this point, Cassandra stages the first of two scenes. This one is the initial point of definition for the story's thematic interests. She loses her temper, thinking her friend has been attacked, and lunges at the young man who had disavowed any responsibility.

"Was it you, you sonofabitch!" Cassandra grabbed his throat and squeezed. "You try to rape my friend?" The guy was able only to shake his head before Wesley took her arm, held it. "Lady, please don't do that. He my cousin," Wesley said.

"I don't give three fucks who he is!" Cassandra said. She began to struggle, but he held both her arms and the more he held her, the calmer she became. Whatever had been in his eyes before Melanie screamed was there no more and she would have given her arms to have it back.

What she thinks she has seen is violence against a woman, but what has actually happened remains unclear—parallel actions have smeared across two adjacent stages. Melanie gets back into Cassandra's car, and the girls drive off, with Cassandra now delivering a diatribe against Melanie's boy-craziness. But the correspondence between Cassandra's own actions and Melanie's has been so coincidental that they don't feel coincidental at all. Out on the street, Cassandra has made a play for a boy, Wesley, and meanwhile, inside the house, Melanie has made a play for another boy and been made the object of unwanted advances tinged around the edges with the beginnings of violence, the kind of violence that Cassandra is known for. The alert reader, having remembered the title, will by now assume that Rhonda Ferguson is offstage being murdered in a flash of male violence.

Cassandra, now behind the wheel of her borrowed automobile, goes on and on and on about boy-craziness and boy-violence. But no one wants to listen. Cassandra is *Cassandra,* after all. So strident is she that Melanie will not attend to her and demands to be let out of the car. Somehow things are patched up. Returning to her neighborhood, Cassandra discovers that Rhonda has indeed been killed (and, sure enough, by her boyfriend), as if Cassandra had predicted this outcome without realizing that it would occur so close to home. At this point Cassandra's entire façade gives way. Without Rhonda's singing voice backing her up and offering her an identity of sorts, Cassandra has no voice at all. And without a voice she has no adult identity whatsoever. On her own stage, as soloist, she can only be mute. After she enters her friend Anita's house, she's ushered into the bedroom and is seated on the bed next to an eyeless old teddy bear.

Out in the living room, Anita's father and her brother are playing chess, and the boy is crowing because he has won, a rarity for him. Meanwhile, in the bedroom, "Anita stood at the foot of the bed, one arm around the bedpost, looking at Cassandra." The only sound in the room is the Big Ben clock. The author is at great pains to give the reader a precise visual and au ditory picture, a sense of where everybody is and what they are hearing, so that we can see as clearly as possible what happens next.

This is Cassandra's second scene, but it is subdued and nearly silent. What she says is an expression of her only desire. "I got to be goin . . . I got to be goin to home." She says this sitting on Anita's bed, the teddy bear behind her. The narrative tells us that Cassandra inflects the word "home" as if it were foreign. As indeed it is, because she has no home, as the story's opening has made clear: both her parents are dead, and, as her teacher told her, Cassandra was "going from pillar to post with no real home." Anita and her mother undress Cassandra as they would a child, and then in the night Anita sings Cassandra to sleep, a kind of lullaby for herself and her friend, her voice "pushing back everything she did not yet understand."

This story is as tightly organized and intricately patterned as any story of its time, but its quiet furious elegance is only evident when the story can be seen as a whole. Its episodes seem arbitrary and meandering when viewed close-up; only when the reader can see the forest do the individual trees make sense, like a painting whose sectioned parts refuse to coalesce until you can see them halfway across the gallery. Cassandra's scenes are all about violence and vulnerability; take her armor off, and you see that she's still a child.

Without those moments in which Cassandra boils over, the reader would be hard put to know the point of the story. Still, Cassandra has gone from pugnacious adult to little child in a day, unheeded at every step, and you can't say you weren't shown how she was forced backward, and you can't say, given her abilities to create a scene, that you weren't warned.

*With many thanks to Andrew Cohen and
Rattawut Lapcharoensap*

Loss of Face

All through this book I have suggested how subtexts may be intimated through the hyperdetailing of gesture, speech, conversational slippage, and scene creation. I want to end with the means by which the soul is usually given away in day-to-day life.

On the other side of Minneapolis from where I live stands the Minneapolis Institute of Arts, which houses among its various collections a portrait, Francisco Goya's *Self-Portrait with Dr. Arrieta,* from 1820. Goya was in his old age when he painted this particular canvas and had recently recovered from an illness during which Dr. Arrieta had cared for him. The painting acknowledges his gratitude with an inscription at the bottom, which in translation reads, "Goya gives thanks to his friend Arrieta for the expert care with which he saved his life from an acute and dangerous illness which he suffered at the close of the year 1819 when he was seventy-three years old. He painted it in 1820."

Dr. Arrieta stands to Goya's right, by the side of the bed, supporting the painter and holding a cup of water or medicine for him to drink. The doctor's face is brightly lit, as if coming out of the darkness, and

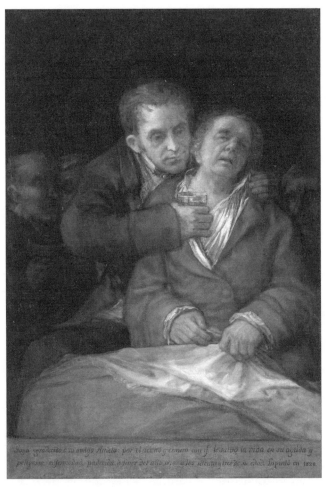

Francisco Goya, Self-Portrait with Dr. Arrieta. *Minneapolis Institute of Arts, The Ethel Morrison Van Derlip Fund*

his face expresses professional forbearance. He looks downward, not at Goya himself—as a doctor, he has seen all this before—and his intelligence and strength of character are visible on his face. This is in contrast to his patient, Goya, whose eyes are shut in pain (a painter presenting himself with his eyes shut is a singularly disturbing image), his expression half in darkness, as if the darkness were eating away at him. His mouth hangs half-open; the bedclothes appear to be slightly soiled. Goya's left hand tugs in a cramped gesture at the bedsheets, a characteristic movement of the dying. The painter presents himself in extremity, as an unheroic person transformed by his sickness, fading into obscurity.

This is the painting's foreground. However, very dimly in the background is the presentation of the painter's subjective world: three demons residing in that darkness, those who haunted Goya during his illness. As the museum catalogue points out, these devils became a distinctive feature of his work after 1788. Without the demons, there is no Goya. The viewer can't have the foreground without the background, the visible without the seemingly invisible, the light without the shadow. In this struggle Dr. Arrieta brings not only his attention to Goya but also, more abstractly, illumination, without which any painter is helpless. He stands with his back to the demons and their punishing subjectivity as a kind of shield against their projective darkness.

The only reason I bring Goya's painting up at all is that I was forced to think about it and the evolution of literary and painterly portraiture generally when I was commenting on a particular scene in a story by a student of mine, some months back, during a conference. The scene my student had written involved two characters. The woman in the scene was giving some bad news to the man. I mentioned in passing that I didn't really know what the guy looked like, and I was curious to know how he was reacting—perhaps, I suggested, the writer might want to describe the expression on the man's face.

"I can't do that," the student said, reluctantly but firmly.

"Why not?" I asked.

There was a pause, as the student—a thoughtful person—tried to explain. He had come up against a wall of some sort. Finally he said, "It's too hard." I was about to say to him that that was really no excuse, that the entire process of writing naturally brings everybody up against what is too hard to do and therefore has to be done, when he interrupted my thoughts by saying, "Besides, no one does that anymore."

Ah, I thought, now *that's* interesting. *Our imagina-*

tions are failing us. In the practice of any art, there are some procedures and practices that artists sometimes forget how to do through neglect or distaste or their inability to concentrate their imaginative forces. My student seemed to be saying that everyone his age had forgotten how to describe faces. Or else they were uncomfortable doing so because of a problem inherent in such descriptions. Something had been given up. The temper of the times resisted it. That particular skill had fallen off the shelf. If it has indeed dropped away from the repertoire of what fiction writers are able to do, we have entered a rather interesting moment in the history of consciousness and of fiction writing.

Before we learn to read words, most of us have started to learn how to read faces, beginning with the mother's or the primary caregiver's face. Most studies of child development posit the age of sixteen weeks as the stage when the infant is able to smile back when someone smiles in his or her direction. By twenty-eight weeks, most infants are already picking up cues from the faces they see, smiling back when smiled upon, frowning when frowned at. By thirty-two weeks the infant may well start crying at the sight of strangers.

An older child's ability to read a face may be, at the most basic level, a survival skill. Particularly in an unstable environment, a child's ability to "read" anger or indifference on the face of an adult may mean the difference between a hot meal or a beating. The more unstable the family, the more a child may need to develop skills in reading faces and gestures just to pull through. These are skills that most of us, of course, never quite give up. In social gatherings, in meetings, and at all stages of love and courtship and trouble, we usually look closely at the faces that we encounter. Everything of importance is to be found there. When you are in a strange location where the people are unknown to you, you are likely to go back to early habits of reading faces, expressions, gestures, in the hope of discovering both character and social subtexts, simply so that you can get by. The face is where you start from. Sometimes that is where you stay.

The idea that a person's character is visible in the face has an old and somewhat odd history. As an idea, it has always been debated from the ancient Greeks onward into the Renaissance. When we look at a person's face, do we think that we are seeing that person's character? Until the late nineteenth and early twentieth centuries, most people thought so. But in these considerations, the beauty or ugliness of a face became a problem that had to be solved. Beautiful people, our reason tells us, do not always have beautiful souls or characters. But sometimes, looking upon beauty, we lose our reason and give to beauty a nobility or depth it does not possess. In his essay "Of Physiognomy," from 1588, Michel de Montaigne writes that nature often does an injustice to noble people by clothing them in ugliness; nevertheless, he says, a beautiful soul is usually visible if one looks closely and steadily enough. *To the beautiful falls the right of command,* he observes, quoting Aristotle, although he adds that this situation is not always just. He then goes on to say that there is an art to distinguishing faces, the kindly ones from the simple ones, the severe from the rough.

In any case, he continues, we should give up our vanities and be straightforward in our expressions (in both senses). Frankness is the best defense, since it disarms others. "I owe my deliverance to my face," Montaigne observes at one point, meaning that his unguardedness has saved him in more than one difficult situation. The pure soul will show itself in the face and in one's actions. Adornments and masks will always fall away, he suggests, and your face will give you away in those moments of helpless spontaneity, so you might as well be straightforward and unadorned and artless in your speech and actions.

What gives Montaigne trouble is the ubiquity of social masks in human interactions. It troubles his particular form of humanism. Almost three hundred years later, Walt Whitman, in *Democratic Vistas* (1871) writes that in the transition from an agrarian to an industrial economy after the Civil War, commerce in American cities has produced an epidemic of unnaturalness and the insincerity of the business class, in which the confidence-man, the trickster, and the seductress would thrive. This change is particularly noticeable in public faces. Everything, he notes, has gone onto a contractual basis. Life has become a theater, and there are *actors* everywhere. Why? Because in a business environment, Whitman asserts, trust is always in jeopardy, and the natural is traded in for the artificial because the natural is the fool's position. The exchange of large sums of money always mitigates against any form of sincerity. Wealth puts people on their guard behind fences and masks, facial neutrality or unreadability. The result is that America breeds its own fakery, with fake aristocrats, false smiles, and phony art. Art, in this environment, Whitman says, is "sophisticated, insane, and its very joy is morbid." To fend off "ruin and dejection" Whitman calls for a "cheerful simplicity," but he does not say how to obtain it. A certain form of innocence, having been lost, has been lost forever, though Whitman can still remember it and summon it, as if it might come back. "Everywhere," he says, sounding like an Old Testament prophet surveying the ruination, there is "an abnormal libidinousness, unhealthy forms, male, female, painted, padded, dyed, chignoned, muddy complexions, bad blood . . . ."

And Whitman had never seen MTV or the Fashion Channel. What he *had* seen was professional masking at work in a mass society. What is bound to arise in a culture of this type is literature about knavery and deceit, particularly deceitful charm, from *The Confidence-Man,* through *Adventures of Huckleberry Finn* up to *The Day of the Locust* and *The Great Gatsby* and beyond them, into our time, a period sometimes described as post-humanist, and which, I am going to suggest, may have become post-face.

We have to return at this point to what is at stake and how to define it, particularly in cultures where faces are mechanically reproduced (on TV or in movies or magazines), commodified, and socially constructed— one would not expect a "cheerful simplicity" to be apparent on Courtney Love's face, nor would we probably welcome it there. It may appear on the president's face, but that is another story, one involving cynical and predatory arrangements. The performer brings a dazzling exterior to whatever show the show happens to be; we, in turn, the viewers, bring to the performance our postmodern arsenal of epistemological skepticism, our irony, our cynicism, our ability to be in on the joke, our occasional wish, knowing there is no "center" anyway, to be swept away. We avoid being fooled by never making a move toward belief unless there is that massive shift in which the totally artificial locates itself in the now-vacated category of the "authentic."

The topic I am dealing with is too large, and too inclined to polemics, probably, to be dealt with sensibly. The problem of the face is really the problem of humanism, and what to do with it in a mass society dominated by manipulative mechanical reproduction. In ordinary life people continue to scan the actual faces of others as much as they ever did. Indeed, our lives are full, sometimes too full, of the information that faces bring to us, from the political realm outward. How do we continue to represent faces in literature and elsewhere, and how do we present such information? *Whose* faces do we put into our stories, and whose faces are we able to read? Some faces we see often, others not at all. We are permitted, even compelled, to see the faces of certain public figures almost every day, but we are not particularly encouraged to see the faces of many others, whom we can describe as the dispossessed, the disinherited, and the vanquished. Sometimes we don't want to see those faces at all because of the demands they place on us. In this way, a literary question quickly becomes a political one.

When we examine a face, what are we looking for? First, as I've already noted, we are trying to get some idea of a person's character. This idea, that a person's basic character can be glimpsed from that person's face, is rare in contemporary American fiction, with some notable exceptions. We have, in a large-scale but tacit social agreement, given up the idea that you can glimpse a person's character from that person's physiognomy, though secretly we may believe that you still can.

Why this is so is complicated by the ubiquity of the actor, as prophesied by Whitman. When I say "famous face," you probably think of Humphrey Bogart, or Greta Garbo, or Audrey Hepburn, Gary Cooper, or Cary Grant. Maybe you think of a politician's face on TV. The portrait of the face, in other words, has been usurped by films and TV just as portraiture was usurped by photography. These faces are usually those of actors. Most of the faces we see on television or in the movies are those of people who are, in effect, playing roles. In this respect, beauty has been contaminated by playacting and by marketing. The face, in this case and in many others, is one weapon in the armory of commerce, a weapon, at its worst, to fool the suckers. We are so used to the idea of everyday masks now that we don't give the matter a second thought. Of course that politician is faking that smile. Who could possibly think otherwise?

The other reason we may have given up the effort to locate a person's *character* based on that person's *appearance* is that the history of racism and the history of disability studies have mostly invalidated this entire epistemological project. Anyone these days is completely justified in feeling squeamish in judging a person's character on the evidence of how that person looks. People are usually not, after all, what they appear to be at first. The game of deducing a person's character from that person's appearance is an old pastime with racists and with those who seek an advantage over the poor or the ugly, the disabled, or any underrepresented minority.

When a new character is introduced in a book, as a rule we all want to know, at least vaguely, what that person looks like. Charles Dickens, for example, tells us immediately. Dickens practiced a characterization in front of a mirror before writing down that character's appearance. But now, in the twenty-first century, we are more likely to be interested in the clothes or the body language than in the face. We are likely to be extremely suspicious of generalizations based on facial descriptions, particularly concerning beauty or its absence. In fact we are likely to be suspicious of any verbal claims about attractiveness. Who is making these claims? We are suspicious, in other words, of our own eagerness to look at something attractive. All claims for beauty or harmony are equally suspicious because any act of observation has a possibly prurient or commercial interest. In this way, every glance becomes ironic. For the most part, readers will tend to get impatient with any lengthy introductory descriptions of facial or physical attributes (except in genre fiction such as romance novels, some historical novels, detective novels, or pornography, where such descriptions still thrive). Irony, a form of self-protection, will trump sincerity in contemporary readers of mainstream fiction, however, almost every time.

Conclusions based on physiognomy and professions of beauty just don't seem plausible anymore; they have acquired a creepy voyeuristic overtone. Even those of us who grew up reading the novels of Thomas Hardy, for example, may cringe, a bit, at this introductory description of Thomasin, from *The Return of the Native,* a novel published in 1878.

> A fair, sweet, and honest country face was revealed, reposing in a nest of wavy chestnut hair. It was between pretty and beautiful. Though her eyes were closed, one could easily imagine the light necessarily shining in them as the culmination of the luminous workmanship around. The groundwork of the face was hopefulness; but over it now lay like a foreign substance a film of anxiety and grief. The grief had been there so shortly as to have abstracted nothing of the bloom, and had as yet but given a dignity to what it might eventually undermine. The scarlet of her lips had not had time to abate, and just now

it appeared still more intense by the absence of the neighbouring and more transient colour of her cheek. The lips frequently parted, with a murmur of words. She seemed to belong rightly to a madrigal—to require viewing through rhyme and harmony.

One thing at least was obvious: she was not made to be looked at thus.

The transactions in this description are weird. Thomasin, who is sleeping, is being looked at by Diggory Venn and by Thomasin's mother, but a third person, the author, also seems to be in the room, and his floating perceptions comprise the substance of the text. The effect is that of a dependable spy standing nearby the main characters and making certain declarations about her. When Eustacia Vye enters the novel a couple of chapters later—she has, the narrator tells us, "the raw material of a divinity," the description of her face alone goes on for three pages. This is narratively courageous and antique. Like the narrators of eighteenth-century English novels, Hardy's storyteller is not afraid to pass on what he believes or to make himself a presence in the implied staging of the novel. The description of Thomasin is particularly notable because emotional assertions are being made about her that the reader can't substantiate. She hasn't yet done anything on the stage of the novel, and the effect of clinical description—she's sleeping and therefore helpless—doubles the discomforting effect of a lingering gaze fixed upon a woman.

Narratively, this is a world we have lost. Yet as a reader I find myself in a guilty position with this description. The air we breathe in that scene has the musty quality of the inside of a museum. Actually, I still admire the bravery of the portrait and am unwilling now to give it an ahistorical correction. But few mainstream writers would describe a character this way now because the entire form of the commentary would provoke suspicion or sarcasm.

Even in Hardy's own time, his descriptive excesses were privately castigated by Henry James. James's own introductory remarks on his characters' faces are much more circumspect. When Isabel Archer is first introduced in *The Portrait of a Lady,* she gets no more than this sentence, as a dog is barking at her feet: ". . . Bunchie's new friend was a tall girl in a black dress, who at first sight looked pretty." That's it. The reader has to wait for a lengthier description. In James, as in life itself, you don't get the full sense of the person at first glance. Only the minor characters get lengthier initial close-ups, for example, that of Lord Warburton whose American face, his physiognomy, reflects a "contented shrewdness." We have not arrived at the grotesque, but we are getting there, by stages.

By the 1920s or 1930s, analysis of character in Anglo-American fiction through physiognomy was almost over, with few exceptions, the portraiture of the grotesque being among them. In Edith Wharton, William Faulkner, Nathanael West, Richard Wright, and Flannery O'Connor, the faces described at length are often squarely in the realm of the unsightly. In English fiction there is a lingering belief in character that can be made visible by physiognomy; this tradition includes Iris Murdoch and Anthony Powell and seems to have something to do with longstanding assumptions about class. But in America, it's as if grotesque faces are expressive even before any expression happens to appear on them.

Beauty begins to be associated with artifice, with Hollywood, in the way that melodies are associated with film sound tracks. In *Gatsby*, there is something fraudulent about Daisy Buchanan's beauty, whereas Wilson's hollow-eyed ugliness is absolutely genuine. Hideous ugliness begins to be associated with the naturally spontaneous and the good, with the final version of this in productions like *The Elephant Man.* Furthermore, because grotesque visages resist readerly irony, they serve as constant ongoing ironic commentaries on their opposites, the intolerably unreal or the untouchably beautiful. Often these grotesque creatures of fiction are, themselves, lookers, compulsive gazers, voyeurs. Popeye, in William Faulkner's *Sanctuary,* from 1931, is a kind of touchstone of Southern Gothic facial anti-ornament. Like many characters in Faulkner defined by self-disgust, he stares, as if he himself were a novelist taking careful notes on a scene and had died in the effort but lived on in a zombie condition. "His face had a queer, bloodless color, as though seen by electric light; against the sunny silence, in his slanted straw hat and his slightly akimbo arms, he had that vicious depthless quality of stamped tin." And, two paragraphs later, "Across the spring Popeye appeared to contemplate him with two knobs of soft black rubber."

Popeye, with his rubberized eyeballs and industrialized face, is not so far away from Flannery O'Connor's description of Hazel Motes sitting on the train in the opening chapter of *Wise Blood* (1962). Hazel's eyes were "the color of pecan shells and set in deep sockets. . . . He had a nose like a shrike's bill . . . his hair looked as if it had been permanently flattened. . . . [The eyes'] settings were so deep that they seemed . . . almost like passages leading somewhere . . . ." As it turns out, Hazel Motes's face is difficult if not impossible to read. No one in the novel can read that face or decipher it. Even by the end of the book, with Hazel's eyesight removed with the spiritual discipline of applications of lye, Mrs. Flood, his landlady, is still trying to see what his face or his eyes might have to say about him once he is safely dead. But (O'Connor seems to insist on this) in his spiritual privacy, Hazel Motes is unreadable by anyone on Earth, and his eyes are still black tunnels that she cannot enter.

Saul Bellow is one of the last holdouts for a tradition of literature portraiture that goes back to Charles Dickens and Henry Fielding and what I'd call the identity theme in the English novel. Like many English novels whose titles derive from the names of their main characters *(Tom Jones, Moll Flanders, Emma, Jane Eyre, David Copperfield),* Bellow's novels often present us with a name—Herzog, Augie March, Ravelstein, or Mr. Sammler—of a character whose complexities will be dramatized at length in the novel named after him. Bellow, like Dickens, is a quick-sketch artist of minor characters, and though these sketches sometimes approach caricature, as they do in the work of another American identity-theme novelist, Sinclair Lewis, Bellow's usually do not arrive there. For the main character, Bellow does a full-length portrait, including the clothes. Bellow holds to the assumption that you can tell who a person is simply by looking at him (or her) carefully enough; if you don't look carefully, you can't get the sense of the person behind the mask.

Here is Valentine Gersbach, from *Herzog.*

> Valentine was a dandy. He had a thick face and heavy jaws; Moses thought he somewhat resembled Putzi Hanfstaengl, Hitler's own pianist. But Gersbach had a pair of extraordinary eyes for a red-haired man, brown, deep, hot eyes, full of life. The lashes, too, were vital, ruddy-dark, long and childlike. And that hair was bearishly thick. Valentine, furthermore, was exquisitely confident of his appearance. You could see it. He knew he was a terribly handsome man. He expected women—all women—to be mad about him.

As we know from reading James Atlas's biography, the real-life victims of Bellow's portraiture have squirmed to discover their faces and characters described on the pages of his novels, but disinterested observers have often remarked on their accuracy. Bellow's good and bad characters are always revealed by their faces; the shrewd observer watches them closely enough to observe the mask falling away every time. There's a predatory gaze in Bellow, a feeling of the *necessity* of watching others. Bellow's novels are full of con-men and intellectual rogues—you have to watch these people in order to get the drop on them. If you don't watch them, they'll prey on you.

Often the Bellow-observer will make a claim about another character that seems dubious, even in retrospect. In *Humboldt's Gift,* for example, the narrator, Charlie Citrine, says of a woman, "You could tell from her eyes that she had slept with too many men." This is the kind of claim that Bellow's narrators usually get away with, and they do it simply by sheer verbal narrative authority. At this point you might doubt Citrine's reliability, and you'd be correct. Bellow's novels negotiate their way through a landscape of large characters, characters who make a difference, who are not overpowered by the systems of which they are a part, and nearly always when a facial portrait appears in a Bellow novel, it is an assessment: it begins with physiological details, moves into character appraisal, and ends with an idea of what that person is worth, in sexual or financial or artistic or purely human terms.

The character or narrator who makes these assessments is often shrewd and unpleasant. You cannot be a nice person and also judge people's characters based on their faces. That requires a kind of cruelty, an ability to say what no one else is willing to say. That is a form of bravery, and Bellow's fiction is always brave in this manner.

But there are signs everywhere of the end of the physiognomy tradition, in the reluctance of American writers to extrapolate character from what a person looks like, as Bellow does. In writers like Don DeLillo, there is the additional suggestion that the individual face simply has no importance anymore, that it is the basis of an antiquarian humanism based on unsound ideas about individuality. If there are no real individuals left, why bother describing their faces? You will have to find something else to describe. Here is a passage from *Mao II,* from 1991: "He knew the boy was standing by the door and he tried to see his face in words, imagine what he looked like, skin and eyes and features, every aspect of that surface called a face, if we can say he has a face, if we believe there is actually something under the hood."

In this passage the face has become the locale for what remains of the wreckage of humanism in a mass culture where disguise has become a norm. The "hood" DeLillo is referring to is the ski-mask hood pulled over the face of a terrorist, meant to disguise an identity. However, when the hood is raised, the face is *still* in question—it is not even a face, just a "something," a vague object among other objects with a vague refer-ent. In DeLillo we enter a world where we cannot re-ally know much of anything, particularly about other people. Other people may have some sort of individual reality, but it is not very likely to appear on their faces or to be visible anywhere else.

The problem of seeing a face, of acknowledging its reality, its connection to a human being who has a separate identity from ours, leads to the problem of obligation, which makes many people uncomfortable. Obligations are often unpleasant and difficult to discharge. This is a point made repeatedly by the French philosopher Emmanuel Levinas in his meditations on the face. If I understand him correctly, Levinas argues that the face is the unique physical presence that provokes the subject's obligations to the Other. The face is not abstract. There would be, by implication, always the necessity therefore to see the face of my enemy, to acknowledge it, and all those to whom I wish to deny a face; my humanity requires such a recognition, particularly in moments of social crisis.

This imperative applies, in a functionally less ethical way, in any social interaction witnessed and dramatized in a novel. We may talk about "faceless" crowds, but the minute we begin to talk about "faceless" fiction or "faceless" characters, particularly in social situations, we are talking about a near-impossibility. In much recent fiction, such as Jennifer Egan's *Look at Me* or Siri Hustvedt's *What I Loved,* there is considerable concentration on what remains of the face, and of what remains of mutual obligation in a narcissistic and psychopathic culture. If the face has turned into a mask, then it is probably our obligation as writers to describe that mask as carefully as we can.

This morning I take my car to the shop for an oil change. The guy who checks the car in is wearing a white shirt and gray cotton pants. His hair is cut fairly short, and he has the bulky body of a former high school or maybe college football player and part-time auto mechanic. He sports a trim blond goatee. He looks respectable, though respectable only recently. The collar of the white shirt seems too tight on his neck. He has a crisp manner of speech and a habit of moving his head back when he finishes a sentence. He looks directly at me when he asks me a question. I don't have to take his measure, but it is my habit, and I do so anyway. But what I really notice about the guy is not his face, but his thick index finger on his right hand because on this finger there is a small tattoo of a screaming skull with hair flying.

Like most people these days, I'm more likely to get an initial sense of who a person is from his accessories, not from his face. What has been emptied out of the face now often appears in the tattoos. Actually, none of my observations make any difference at all if our interaction goes smoothly, if my car's oil is changed, and I pay the bill. If there's no tension, no plus or minus, then who cares what anybody looks like? Only when tensions arise, when we fall in love or are threatened or coerced, do faces and clothes and tattoos and personal details begin to count.

Such tensions begin with social uneasiness of the sort we all have felt at various times in the company of people we do not entirely trust. Then they start to escalate, especially when we are attracted to someone or feel physically or psychically threatened. The more confined the dramatic space, the more likely it is that facial expressions will become important. One of the greatest writers—perhaps the greatest—of social uneasiness is Marcel Proust, for whom social anxiety is a constant source of inspiration. Proust is equally good on smugness and social *un*concern, but his comic sense is most likely to appear whenever a character's fears give himself away, as in his description of Dr. Cottard, in *Swann's Way*, in the translation by Moncrieff, Kilmartin, and Enright.

> Dr. Cottard was never quite certain of the tone in which he ought to reply to any observation, or whether the speaker was jesting or in earnest. And so by way of precaution he would embellish all his facial expressions with the offer of a conditional, a provisional smile whose expectant subtlety would exonerate him from the charge of being a simpleton, if the

remark addressed to him should turn out to have been facetious. But as he must also be prepared to face the alternative, he dared not allow this smile to assert itself positively on his features, and you would see there a perpetually flickering uncertainty, in which could be deciphered the question that he never dared to ask: "Do you really mean that?" He was no more confident of the manner in which he ought to conduct himself in the street, or indeed in life generally, than he was in a drawing-room; and he might be seen greeting passers-by, carriages, and anything that occurred with a knowing smile which absolved his subsequent behaviour of all impropriety, since it proved, if it should turn out unsuited to the occasion, that he was well aware of that, and that if he had assumed a smile, the jest was a secret of his own.

In this example we're not being offered the whole of Dr. Cottard's face, but only his smile. Cottard's face has been segmented, and in this process his nervous smile has come to define him. Insecurity is his social essence. It's a Cheshire-Cat maneuver. What is characteristic substitutes for character; the smile suffices because Dr. Cottard's worries about appearing to be stupid and naïve in mixed company trump everything else about him. One feature of a character's face viewed at the right moment and from the right angle reveals the necessary subtext, the subterranean worries; it's as if the nervous smile is the corridor to the unsaid. Such moments do not define an entire character and are not meant to. We don't get physiognomy as an index to character. Instead, these moments define a position or stance in a tense social interaction. We're not talking about character anymore, but social-behavior patterns.

Paula Fox is one of our contemporary masters of such moments (Andrea Barrett has justly described her fiction as "Proustian"), and the introductory section of Fox's novel *The Widow's Children* is full of these dramatic stagings in which parts of the face give a sense of what's going on underneath, which is usually dire. At the beginning of that novel, the situation is this: Clara, an insecure daughter, is going to a hotel for drinks with her wickedly indifferent mother, Laura, Laura's alcoholic husband, Desmond, her brother Carlos, who is gay, and Laura's friend (but not lover) Peter Rice, a downcast book editor. Laura, we later discover, is holding onto a secret, namely that her own mother, Alma, has just died the day before.

The tension in the scene is remarkable. Everyone is trying to relax, but, thanks in part to Laura's diabolic cleverness and to too much alcohol and a concatenation of secrets, everyone in the room is keyed up, spiteful, and affrighted. There is an air of untamed free-floating maliciousness, which can descend on anyone at any time. It is like a cocktail party of savagely clever and malevolent dragons.

You might think that facial expressions are dramatically free of the settings in which they appear, but no. The setting has a way of determining everything in scenes like this. What the opening of Paula Fox's novel emphasizes here is that facial expressions become most important when the dramatic spaces have collapsed or become agonizingly confined. There's nowhere else to look. All the other important information has been removed, and we are inside the social novel, with a vengeance. With the crowding of characters, you are forced to see people close-up and to look straight at them minute after minute in a no-exit setting, a terribly confined space, like the hotel room of this opening section, or a bus, or a jail cell—any place where people have managed to get themselves confined and cannot, for one reason or another, get themselves out. You parse their faces so closely under such grievously tense circumstances that the faces themselves start to show the strain and then begin to be segmented.

In *The Widow's Children* examples of segmented faces proliferate, with a particular concentration on eyes and mouths. Laura looks at her husband with "mirror eyes." Clara arrives at the hotel and is greeted by Desmond's "wasted smile." When Laura and Carlos look at Clara, she has the impression of "two eagles swooping toward her," with the same "deep set eyes above massive lid folds," of something "not quite human in the eyes above their smiling lips." Desmond has a black mustache and "lips like old rubber bands." When Peter Rice enters the book, he is given an almost old-fashioned entrance, suitable for his old-fashioned courtliness: "His thin hair was gray, his features narrow, and from behind his glasses, his pale blue eyes gazed out mildly. He gave the impression of being clean and dry as though he had been pressed between two large blotters which had absorbed all his vital juices."

As the scene continues, we begin to notice all the details about faces latched onto details about gestures. We also get details about the exact manner in which things are said, from whispers to strangled shouts. This is a fully *staged* novel. That is, the staging in it is so detailed that you could cast it, put the actors on the stage, block out their movements, and indicate the directions for line readings from the narrative alone, but the emphasis on the staging is meant to emphasize not just the surface but the subtext and the sense of claustrophobia. The details about faces and gestures begin to pile up: Laura's cheek, when Peter embraced her, had been "dry, powdery. It was what he had come to desire, all things dry, ash, dead leaf, stone." Facial expressions start to be compounded and mixed: Desmond has on his face an expression that was both "truculent and timid," and Laura, in a angry moment, has eyes "crinkled with laughter." Peter's face, in a moment of panic, "looked oddly stretched as though he were holding it in front of him with taut hands." Clara feels her own face contorting into a "hideous smile of malice." Readers who are particularly attentive might notice how often, in these descriptions, the eyes contradict the lips; the face itself forms a sort of expressive double negative, hideous smiles or cheerful frowns.

Paula Fox seems to know more than any other contemporary American writer about the danger of facial signals—how subtexts can be loaded onto something as initially innocent as a smile; how a smile can transform, in a moment, into a seizure of malice, as with Laura's smile in a frightening close-up, "the three plump cushions of her lips, the large, somewhat dingy teeth, and behind them the quivering mucosity of her tongue."

During a visit that Paula Fox made to the University of Michigan MFA program in writing, one of the graduate students asked her, speaking of this scene in *The Widow's Children*, how it was that she had learned to write with such intensity about the seemingly small details. Where, the student wanted to know, had she learned to employ this effect of hyperattention to faces and gestures? She replied that it was more than a writerly technique. She had been an unwanted child, she said, handed from one foster parent to another and had never been sure where her next meal would come from. When she was in her mother's presence, she never knew whether she would be exiled without dinner or fawned upon or have a drink thrown at her. "It made me watchful," she said. "My habit of watchfulness went into that book."

Fiction once *began* with the face, with the act of observation of the faces of others. Does it still? It's arguable. I can imagine a skeptic wondering what difference it makes whether writers describe faces or not. Does anything of importance really hang in the balance? Who cares? Does it make any difference to the operations of the world? Who cares about the face anymore? Is reading the face still a survival skill, as Paula Fox suggested, and if so, for whom?

In Anton Chekhov's novella "The Story of a Nobody," the narrator observes that in St. Petersburg, a true face is not required: "there is no need to describe commonplace looks . . . men's looks here have no significance even in matters of love."

As it happens, both inside literature's examples and outside of them, the face is still where we are answerable to our emotions and to our obligations. If Levinas claims that the face is where acknowledgment and obligation start and the face is never abstract, still, some adults eventually lose that particular skill quite willingly. The face of the other becomes *inconvenient.* Under these circumstances, the faces of the innocent, the vanquished, the weak, and the lost don't have to be looked at or their humanity acknowledged. Why bother with them? They're losers.

At the present historical moment our obsession with beauty has become pernicious and ideological. Beauty has been co-opted everywhere by marketing. Montaigne would tell us that ugly unphotogenic people may be tender and wise persons whose presence we require in the stories of our lives. What starts at the intimately personal eventually enlarges. In any moment of love or betrayal, tension and threat, sorrow or depression or grief, or even moments of political decision, at what do we look, if not the face? What, or whom, do we recognize there?

If we do not see the Other, do we still count ourselves as civilized? If so, on what basis? The small person must by necessity learn to read the face of the large person to survive. But the strong are under no necessity to acknowledge the faces of the weak; if they do so, it is for the sake of recognizing something of humanity in those who might otherwise be invisible.

A final question: if we take away the face and the subtext, then where is the story? Maybe in the clothes, or the weapons, or the cars, and the explosions and the shoes, and the swimming pools and the sex and the firepower and the situation, in a kind of reproduction of the glittering surfaces and the beasts of commerce that feed on them. But if the story is going to be a story about persons who have been granted their humanity, who can live and die with all their attendant angels and devils lurking in the background, people, in short, with those archaic things called souls, it probably cannot do without that *something*—let's call it a face and not be embarrassed about it—that lies underneath the hood.

Here is the story of a face, then, in one paragraph, from John Cheever's *Journals,* which seems to say it all, as a young ugly man combs his hair to meet someone arriving on a train.

> And there is the face, which is the most important experience for me and which seems to escape me. I am waiting for someone to arrive on the train. It is toward the end of the afternoon. The train is late. The taxi driver leaves his cab. He is youngish. There is really nothing very specific about him. He is, I think, ugly. If he ever went to a dance—which I doubt he would—he would have trouble getting a date. So, to this stranger, whom I very likely will never see again, I bring a bulky and extended burden of anxieties like the baggage train of some early army. Does he live with his wife, his girl, his mother, his drunken father? Does he live alone? Does he have a small bank ac-

count, a big cock, is his underwear clean? Does he throw low dice, has he paid his dentist's bills—or has he ever been to the dentist's? We see the light of the approaching train in the distance, burning gratuitously in the full light of day. At this sight, he takes a comb out of his pocket and runs it through his hair. . . . What I do see in this gesture is the man—his essence, his independence; see in his homely face the beauty of a velocity that does not apprehend the angle of repose. Here in this gesture of combing his hair is a marvel of self-possession, and the thrill is mutual and is, it seems, the key to this time of life.

Books referred to and recommended:

Atxaga, Bernardo: *Obabakoak* (trans. Margaret Jull Costa)

Auster, Paul: *The Invention of Solitude*

Bausch, Richard: *The Stories of Richard Bausch*

Bellow, Saul: *Herzog: Humboldt's Gift*

Borges, Jorge Luis: *Fictions* (trans. Andrew Hurley)

Brennan, Maeve: *The Springs of Affection*

Brooks, Peter: *Reading for the Plot*

Cather, Willa: *My Mortal Enemy*

Cheever, John: *The Stories of John Cheever; The Journals of John Cheever*

Chekhov, Anton: *The Steppe and Other Stories* (trans. Ronald Wilks); *Plays* (trans. Laurence Senelick)

Coetzee, J. M.: *Disgrace*

Delbanco, Nicholas: *What Remains*

DeLillo, Don: *Mao II*

Dostoyevsky, Fyodor: *Crime and Punishment* (trans. Jesse Coulson); *The Brothers Karamazov* (trans. David McDuff)

Egan, Jennifer: *Look at Me*

Ellroy, James: *My Dark Places*

Faulkner, William: *Sanctuary; The Sound and the Fury*

Fitzgerald, B. H.: *Early Occult Memory Systems of the Lower Midwest: Poems*

Fitzgerald, F. Scott: *The Great Gatsby*

Fitzgerald, Penelope: *The Blue Flower*

Fox, Paula: *The Widow's Children*
Freud, Sigmund: *Writings on Art and Literature*
    (ed. Strachey)
Frost, Robert: *The Complete Poems*
Gaddis, William: *The Recognitions*
Gide, André: *La Symphonie pastorale*
Green, Henry: *Loving; Living; Party Going*
Hardy, Thomas: *The Return of the Native*
Hass, Robert: *Twentieth Century Pleasures*
Hofmannstahl, Hugo von: *Selected Prose* (trans. Mary
    Hottinger, and Tania and James Stern)
Hornby, Nick: *High Fidelity*
James, Henry: "In the Cage"; "The Turn of the Screw";
    The Sacred Fount
Jones, Edward P.: *Lost in the City*
Joyce, James: *Dubliners*
Kafka, Franz: *The Castle* (trans. Mark Harman)
Kierkegaard, Søren: *Philosophical Fragments* (trans. Edna
    and Howard Hong)
Koeppen, Wolfgang: *Death in Rome; The Hothouse* (trans.
    Michael Hofmann)
Kushner, Tony: *Angels in America*
Lowry, Malcolm: *Under the Volcano*
McPherson, James Alan: *Crabcakes*
Melville, Herman: *Moby-Dick*
Montaigne, Michel de: *Essays* (trans. M. A. Screech)
Moore, Lorrie: *Self-Help; Like Life*
O'Connor, Flannery: *The Complete Stories; Wise Blood*
O'Neill, Eugene: *Long Day's Journey into Night*
Percy, Walker: *The Moviegoer; Lancelot*

Pinter, Harold: *Old Times*
Porter, Katherine Anne: *The Collected Stories*
Powers, J. F.: *The Stories of J. F. Powers*
Prose, Francine: *Reading like a Writer; A Changed Man*
Rilke, Rainer Maria: *The Notebooks of Malte Laurids Brigge*
    (trans. Stephen Mitchell)
Saunders, George: *Pastoralia*
Stone, Robert: *Bear and His Daughter*
Trevor, William: *The Collected Stories*
Ueland, Brenda: *If You Want to Write*
White, Patrick: *Voss*
Whitman, Walt: *Democratic Vistas*

The text of *The Art of Subtext* is set in Warnock Pro, a typeface designed by Robert Slimbach for Adobe Systems in 2000. Book design by Wendy Holdman. Composition by Prism Publishing Center. Manufactured by Versa Press on acid-free paper.

CHARLES BAXTER is the author of a dozen books, including the novels *The Soul Thief* and *The Feast of Love,* a finalist for the National Book Award; the short-story collections *Gryphon: New and Selected Stories* and *A Relative Stranger;* and the essay collection *Burning Down the House: Essays on Fiction.* He is also the editor of *Sherwood Anderson: Collected Stories,* published by the Library of America. He currently teaches at the University of Minnesota and lives in Minneapolis.